365 Bible Promises for People Who Worry
(a little or a lot)

365 BIBLE PROMISES

for People Who Worry

(a little or a lot)

ALICE CHAPIN

Living Books®
Tyndale House Publishers, Inc.
Wheaton, Illinois

CONTENTS

PREFACE

Everyone worries about something at times, either a little or a lot. Money problems. Illness. Children's needs. Some of life's difficulties are potential grounds for worry. After a bout of worry, we often find appropriate Scriptures that would have helped, had we known where to look.

In *365 Bible Promises for People Who Worry (a little or a lot)*, you'll find carefully chosen Scriptures already written out that match certain worries common to everyone. So, no more searching. Serious problems rarely have quick fixes, but recalling Bible verses that "just fit" a certain problem can boost faith, uplift the spirit, and comfort. The Bible, after all, is the source of knowledge about the abundant life that Jesus talked about.

I hope with all my heart that the verses I have selected will help contemporary Christians dispel discouragement and give hope in the midst of a myriad of day-to-day struggles that pit worry against strong faith.

When I read these verses, I often walk away whistling. Maybe you will, too.

—ALICE CHAPIN

I WORRY ABOUT MONEY

☐ 1 _____

Enjoy prosperity while you can. But when hard times strike, realize that both come from God. That way you will realize that nothing is certain in this life. (Ecclesiastes 7:14)

T A K E A W A Y
Anybody who thinks money is everything has never been sick. Or is.—Malcolm S. Forbes

☐ 2 _____

Godliness with contentment is great gain. (1 Timothy 6:6, KJV)

T A K E A W A Y
He who desires nothing but God is rich and happy.—Alphonsus Liguori

[Job fell to the ground before God after hearing of the deaths of his children and livestock and said,] "Naked came I out of my mother's womb, and naked shall I return thither: The LORD gave, and the LORD hath taken away; blessed be the name of the LORD." (Job 1:21, KJV)

T A K E A W A Y
I [the apostle Paul] have learned, in whatsoever state I am, therewith to be content. (Philippians 4:11, KJV)

☐ 4 _____

Give me neither poverty nor riches! Give me just enough to satisfy my needs. ❖ For the love of money is the root of all evil. ❖ To enjoy your work and to accept your lot in life—that is indeed a gift from God. The person who does that will not need to look back with sorrow on his past, for God gives him joy. (Proverbs 30:8; 1 Timothy 6:10, KJV; Ecclesiastes 5:20, TLB)

T A K E A W A Y
To enjoy your work and to accept your lot in life is indeed a gift from God.

☐ 5 _____

Do not love the world or the things in the world. ❖ The Lord is a strong fortress. The godly run to him and are safe. The rich man thinks of his wealth as an impregnable defense, a high wall of safety.

What a dreamer! ❖ God is our refuge and strength, a tested help in times of trouble. (1 John 2:15, NKJV; Proverbs 18:10-11; Psalm 46:1, TLB)

TAKEAWAY
Wealth is not an impregnable defense. The Lord is a strong fortress. The godly run to him and are safe.

☐ 6 _____

Don't worry about everyday life—whether you have enough food, drink, and clothes. Doesn't life consist of more than food and clothing? . . . And if God cares so wonderfully for flowers that are here today and gone tomorrow, won't he more surely care for you? . . . Why be like the pagans who are so deeply concerned about these things? Your heavenly Father already knows all your needs, and he will give you all you need from day to day if you live for him and make the Kingdom of God your primary concern. (Matthew 6:25, 30-33)

TAKEAWAY
Your heavenly Father already knows all your needs.

☐ 7 _____

Wise men and fools alike spend their lives scratching for food, and never seem to get enough. Both have the same problem, yet the poor man who is wise lives a far better life. ❖ To be wise is as good as being rich; in fact, it is better. (Ecclesiastes 6:7-8; 7:11, TLB)

3

Those who love money will never have enough.
. . . The more you have, the more people come to
help you spend it. So what is the advantage of
wealth—except perhaps to watch it run through
your fingers! (Ecclesiastes 5:10-11)

POWERTHOUGHT Your heavenly Father knows that
you need all these things. But seek first the kingdom of God
and His righteousness, and all these things shall be added to
you. Therefore do not worry about tomorrow.—Matthew
6:32-34, NKJV

Two

I WORRY ABOUT MY
TROUBLES: WHY ME?

☐ 8 _____

My sighs are many, and my heart is faint. ❖ These
trials are only to test your faith, to show that it is
strong and pure. It is being tested as fire tests and
purifies gold—and your faith is far more precious to
God than mere gold. So if your faith remains strong
after being tried by fiery trials, it will bring you
much praise and glory and honor on the day when
Jesus Christ is revealed to the whole world.❖ Do
not throw away this confident trust in the Lord, no
matter what happens. Remember the great reward it
brings you! (Lamentations 1:22, KJV; 1 Peter 1:7;
Hebrews 10:35)

TAKEAWAY
Scar tissue most often becomes the skin's tough-
est and strongest part.

I have chosen thee in the furnace of affliction.
❖ I spake unto thee in thy prosperity; but thou
saidst, I will not hear. ❖ Don't you realize how kind,
tolerant, and patient God is with you? Or don't you
care? Can't you see how kind he has been in giving
you time to turn from your sin? ❖ But the LORD still
waits for you to come to him so he can show you
his love and compassion. For the LORD is a faithful
God. Blessed are those who wait for him to help
them. (Isaiah 48:10; Jeremiah 22:21, KJV; Romans
2:4; Isaiah 30:18)

> TAKEAWAY
> **As many as I love, I rebuke and chasten: be zealous
> therefore, and repent. Behold, I stand at the door,
> and knock. (Revelation 3:19-20, KJV)**

All praise to the God and Father of our Lord Jesus
Christ. He is the source of every mercy and the God
who comforts us. He comforts us in all our troubles
so that we can comfort others. When others are troubled, we will be able to give them the same comfort
God has given us. You can be sure that the more we
suffer for Christ, the more God will shower us with
his comfort through Christ. (2 Corinthians 1:3-5)

> TAKEAWAY
> **When others are troubled and need sympathy
> and encouragement, we can pass on to them the
> same help and comfort that God has given us.**

_____

Whenever trouble comes your way, let it be an opportunity for joy. For when your faith is tested, your endurance has a chance to grow. So let it grow, for when your endurance is fully developed, you will be strong in character and ready for anything. (James 1:2-4)

> *TAKEAWAY*
> How frail is humanity! How short is life, and how full of trouble! ❖ The LORD also will be a refuge for the oppressed, a refuge in times of trouble. (Job 14:1; Psalm 9:9, KJV)

☐ 12 _____

Dear friends, don't be bewildered or surprised when you go through the fiery trials ahead. . . . These trials will make you partners with Christ in his suffering. ❖ [The Roman soldiers] led him away to crucify him. ❖ He was oppressed, and he was afflicted, yet he opened not his mouth. (1 Peter 4:12-13, TLB; Matthew 27:31; Isaiah 53:7, KJV)

> *TAKEAWAY*
> Christ's suffering was always a solid fact to me, something I believed but never really felt . . . *until* I myself experienced terrible pain, unbearable suffering, in an awful car accident. Then, his pain became mine.—A Florida woman

☐ 13 _____

Two sisters [Mary and Martha] sent a message to Jesus telling him, "Lord, the one you love is very sick." But when Jesus heard about it he said, "Lazarus's sickness will not end in death. No, it is for the glory of God. I, the Son of God, will receive glory from this.". . . When Jesus arrived at Bethany, he was told that Lazarus had already been in his grave for four days. . . . Then Jesus shouted, "Lazarus, come out!" And Lazarus came out, bound in graveclothes, his face wrapped in a headcloth. Jesus told them, "Unwrap him and let him go!" Many of the people who were with Mary believed in Jesus when they saw this happen. (John 11:3-4, 17, 43-45)

TAKEAWAY
Call upon me in the day of trouble: I will deliver thee, and thou shalt glorify me. (Psalm 50:15, KJV)

☐ 14 _____

We can rejoice, too, when we run into problems and trials, for we know that they are good for us—they help us learn to endure. And endurance develops strength of character in us, and character strengthens our confident expectation of salvation. And this expectation will not disappoint us. For we know how dearly God loves us, because he has given us the Holy Spirit to fill our hearts with his love. (Romans 5:3-5)

TAKEAWAY
Job was a righteous man, yet Job suffered. Job learned through his suffering to see God as his place of refuge, sufficient in times of trouble.

POWERTHOUGHT

I asked the Lord, that I might grow
    In faith, and love, and every grace;
Might more of His salvation know,
    And seek more earnestly His face.

I hoped that in some favoured hour
    At once He'd answer my request,
And by His love's constraining power
    Subdue my sins, and give me rest.

Instead of this, He made me feel
    The hidden evils of my heart;
And let the angry powers of hell
    Assault my soul in every part.

Yea more, with His own hand He seemed
    Intent to aggravate my woe;
Crossed all the fair designs I schemed,
    Blasted my gourds, and laid me low.

"Lord, why is this?" I trembling cried,
    "Wilt thou pursue Thy worm to death?"
"'Tis in this way," the Lord replied,
    "I answer prayer for grace and faith.

"These inward trials I employ
    From self and pride to set thee free;
And break thy schemes of earthly joy,
    That thou may'st seek thy all in Me."

—JOHN NEWTON

Three

I WORRY ABOUT MAKING A DECISION

☐ 15 _____

Trust in the LORD with all your heart; do not depend on your own understanding. Seek his will in all you do, and he will direct your paths. ❖ Grow in the special favor and knowledge of our Lord and Savior Jesus Christ. ❖ Let the words of Christ, in all their richness, live in your hearts and make you wise. Use his words to teach and counsel each other. (Proverbs 3:5-6; 2 Peter 3:18; Colossians 3:16)

TAKEAWAY
In everything you do, put God first. He will direct your paths.

☐ 16 _____

If you need wisdom—if you want to know what God wants you to do—ask him, and he will gladly tell you. He will not resent your asking. But when

you ask him, be sure that you really expect him to
answer, for a doubtful mind is as unsettled as a wave
of the sea that is driven and tossed by the wind.
❖ In him lie hidden all the treasures of wisdom and
knowledge. (James 1:5-6; Colossians 2:3)

T A K E A W A Y
**Ask God what he wants you to do. He will gladly
tell you.**

☐ 17 _____

The glory of the young is their strength; the gray
hair of experience is the splendor of the old. ❖ The
godly offer good counsel; they know what is right
from wrong. (Proverbs 20:29; Psalm 37:30)

T A K E A W A Y
The godly man is a good counselor.

☐ 18 _____

I have commanded you today to love the LORD
your God and to keep his commands, laws, and
regulations by walking in his ways. If you do this,
you will live and become a great nation, and the
LORD your God will bless you and the land you are
about to enter and occupy. . . . I have given you
the choice between life and death, between blessings and curses. I call on heaven and earth to witness the choice you make. Oh, that you would
choose life, that you and your descendants might
live! Choose to love the LORD your God and to
obey him and commit yourself to him, for he is
your life. (Deuteronomy 30:16, 19-20)

TAKEAWAY
I have given you the choice between life and
death, between blessings and curses. I call on
heaven and earth to witness the choice you make.

☐ 19 _____

Behold, I have longed after thy precepts: quicken
me in thy righteousness. Let thy mercies come also
unto me, O LORD, even thy salvation, according to
thy word. So shall I have wherewith to answer him
that reproacheth me: for I trust in thy word. And
take not the word of truth utterly out of my mouth;
for I have hoped in thy judgments. . . . Teach me
good judgment and knowledge: for I have believed
thy commandments. . . . Thy word is a lamp unto
my feet, and a light unto my path. (Psalm 119:40-
43, 66, 105, KJV)

TAKEAWAY
I seek thy precepts, O LORD. Thy word is a light
unto my path.

☐ 20 _____

The steps of good men are directed by the Lord.
He delights in each step they take. ❖ You will keep
on guiding me all my life with your wisdom and
counsel, and afterwards receive me into the glories
of heaven! (Psalms 37:23; 73:24, TLB)

TAKEAWAY
The steps of good men are directed by the Lord.

The LORD says, "I will guide you along the best pathway for your life. I will advise you and watch over you. Do not be like a senseless horse or mule that needs a bit and bridle to keep it under control." Many sorrows come to the wicked, but unfailing love surrounds those who trust the LORD. (Psalm 32:8-10)

TAKEAWAY

We can gather our thoughts, but the LORD gives the right answer. (Proverbs 16:1)

POWERTHOUGHT   The glory of great men must always be measured against the means they have used to acquire it.—FRANÇOIS DE LA ROCHEFOUCAULD, *Maxims*

Four

I WORRY ABOUT WHAT OTHERS THINK OF ME

☐ 22 _____

The LORD said to Samuel, "Don't judge by his appearance or height, for I have rejected him. The LORD doesn't make decisions the way you do! People judge by outward appearance, but the LORD looks at a person's thoughts and intentions." (1 Samuel 16:7)

> *TAKEAWAY*
> **Men judge by outward appearance, but God looks at a man's thoughts and intentions.**

☐ 23 _____

You have been set apart for God. You have been made right with God because of what the Lord Jesus Christ and the Spirit of our God have done for you. ❖ Our lives are a fragrance presented by Christ to God. But this fragrance is perceived differently by those being saved and by those perishing. (1 Corinthians 6:11; 2 Corinthians 2:15)

TAKEAWAY
God has set the members, each one of them, in the body just as He pleased. (1 Corinthians 12:18, NKJV)

☐ 24 _____

He died for everyone so that those who receive his new life will no longer live to please themselves. . . . So we have stopped evaluating others by what the world thinks about them. (2 Corinthians 5:15-16)

TAKEAWAY
He died for all.

☐ 25 _____

Remember, dear brothers and sisters, that few of you were wise in the world's eyes, or powerful, or wealthy when God called you. Instead, God deliberately chose things the world considers foolish in order to shame those who think they are wise. And he chose those who are powerless to shame those who are powerful. God chose things despised by the world, things counted as nothing at all, and used them to bring to nothing what the world considers important, so that no one can ever boast in the presence of God. (1 Corinthians 1:26-29)

God has chosen to use ideas (and people) the world considers foolish to shame those people considered by the world as wise and great.

☐ 26 _____

The rich and the poor have this in common: The LORD made them both. ❖ [Jesus said,] "Real life is not measured by how much we own. . . . Yes, a person is a fool to store up earthly wealth but not have a rich relationship with God." (Proverbs 22:2; Luke 12:15, 21)

TAKEAWAY
The rich and the poor have this in common: The LORD made them both.

☐ 27 _____

There is no longer Jew or Greek, there is no longer slave or free, there is no longer male and female; for all of you are one in Christ Jesus. (Galatians 3:28, NRSV)

TAKEAWAY
Cure yourself to the inclination to bother about how you look to other people. Be concerned only with the idea God has of you.—Miguel de Unamuno

☐ 28 _____

The greatest among you must be a servant. But those who exalt themselves will be humbled, and

those who humble themselves will be exalted.
(Matthew 23:11-12)

TAKEAWAY
The more lowly your service to others, the greater you are.

POWERTHOUGHT All ground is level at the foot of the cross.—GEN. ROBERT E. LEE

Five

I WORRY ABOUT
DEATH AND DYING

☐ 29 _____

Yea, though I walk through the valley of the
shadow of death, I will fear no evil: for thou art
with me; thy rod and thy staff they comfort me.
(Psalm 23:4, KJV)

TAKEAWAY
As the last bell struck, a peculiar sweet smile
shone over his face, and he lifted up his head a
little, and quickly said "Adsum!" and fell back. It
was the word we used at school, when names
were called, and lo, he, whose heart was that of a
little child, had answered to his name, and stood
in the presence of the Master.—William Make-
peace Thackeray, speaking of Colonel Newcome
in *The Newcomes*

☐ 30 _____

We have redemption through [Jesus'] blood, the forgiveness of sins. ❖ He who believes in Him is not
condemned; but he who does not believe is condemned already. (Colossians 1:14; John 3:18, NKJV)

TAKEAWAY
We have forgiveness through His blood.

☐ 31 _____

As Moses lifted up the serpent in the wilderness,
even so must the Son of man be lifted up: that whosoever believeth in him should not perish, but have
eternal life. For God so loved the world, that he
gave his only begotten Son, that whosoever
believeth in him should not perish, but have everlasting life. (John 3:14-16, KJV)

TAKEAWAY
Whoever believes in Jesus will have eternal life.

☐ 32 _____

[Jesus said,] "Don't be troubled. You trust God, now
trust in me. There are many rooms in my Father's
home, and I am going to prepare a place for you. If
this were not so, I would tell you plainly. When
everything is ready, I will come and get you, so that
you will always be with me where I am."(John 14:1-3)

TAKEAWAY
**How great, how lovely, how certain is the knowl-
edge of all things there [in heaven], with no error
and no trouble, where the wisdom of God shall**

be imbibed at its very source with no difficulty
and with utmost happiness!—Augustine of Hippo

☐ 33 _____

We are looking forward to the new heavens and
new earth he has promised, a world where everyone
is right with God. ❖ I heard a loud shout from the
throne, saying, "Look, the home of God is now
among his people! He will live with them, and they
will be his people. God himself will be with them.
He will remove all of their sorrows, and there will
be no more death or sorrow or crying or pain. For
the old world and its evils are gone forever."
(2 Peter 3:13; Revelation 21:3-4)

TAKEAWAY
**Death cannot harm me because it is a stingless
bee; its stinger is lodged in Christ.**—Peter J.
Kreeft, *Love Is Stronger Than Death*

☐ 34 _____

The fact is that Christ has been raised from the
dead. He has become the first of a great harvest of
those who will be raised to life again. . . . Everyone
dies because all of us are related to Adam, the first
man. But all who are related to Christ, the other
man, will be given new life. . . . But someone may
ask, "How will the dead be raised? What kind of
bodies will they have?" What a foolish question!
When you put a seed into the ground, it doesn't
grow into a plant unless it dies first. And what you
put in the ground is not the plant that will grow, but

only a dry little seed of wheat or whatever it is you are planting. Then God gives it a new body—just the kind he wants it to have. A different kind of plant grows from each kind of seed. (1 Corinthians 15:20, 22, 35-38)

TAKEAWAY

Our earthly bodies, which die and decay, will be different when they are resurrected, for they will never die. Our bodies now disappoint us, but when they are raised, they will be full of glory. (1 Corinthians 15:42-43)

☐ 35 _____

They shall mock him, and shall scourge him, and shall spit upon him, and shall kill him: and the third day he shall rise again. ❖ He will swallow up death in victory. . . . This is our God. (Mark 10:34, Isaiah 25:8-9, KJV)

TAKEAWAY

We shall all be changed. (1 Corinthians 15:51, KJV)

POWERTHOUGHT My resurrection is quite a thrilling event to ponder! Me! Raised up from the dead!

Six

I WORRY ABOUT
PAST MISTAKES

☐ 36 _____

There is not a righteous man on earth who continually does good and who never sins. ❖ For all have sinned and fall short of the glory of God. (Ecclesiastes 7:20; Romans 3:23, NASB)

> **TAKEAWAY**
> *All* **have sinned, not just me!**

☐ 37 _____

When you came to Christ, . . . it was a spiritual procedure—the cutting away of your sinful nature. . . . He canceled the record that contained the charges against us. He took it and destroyed it by nailing it to Christ's cross. In this way, God disarmed the evil rulers and authorities. He shamed them publicly by his victory over them on the cross of Christ. (Colossians 2:11, 14-15)

TAKEAWAY
When you came to Christ, he blotted out the charges against you.

☐ 38 _____

If we say we have no sin, we are only fooling ourselves and refusing to accept the truth. But if we confess our sins to him, he is faithful and just to forgive us and to cleanse us from every wrong. (1 John 1:8-9)

TAKEAWAY
If we confess our sins to him, he can be depended on to forgive us and to cleanse us.

☐ 39 _____

[Paul said,] "Brothers, listen! In this man Jesus there is forgiveness for your sins. Everyone who believes in him is freed from all guilt and declared right with God—something the Jewish law could never do." (Acts 13:38-39)

TAKEAWAY
Everyone who trusts in Jesus is freed from guilt and declared righteous.

☐ 40 _____

For God so loved the world that he gave his only Son, so that everyone who believes in him will not

perish but have eternal life. God did not send his
Son into the world to condemn it, but to save it.
There is no judgment awaiting those who trust him.
But those who do not trust him have already been
judged for not believing in the only Son of God.
(John 3:16-18)

TAKEAWAY

**God gave his only Son. Anyone who believes in
him shall not perish but have eternal life.**

☐ 41 _____

Long ago, even before he made the world, God
loved us and chose us in Christ to be holy and without fault in his eyes. ❖ Oh, what joy for those
whose rebellion is forgiven, whose sin is put out of
sight! (Ephesians 1:4; Psalm 32:1)

TAKEAWAY

**Through what Christ did for us, we are made
holy in God's eyes, without a single fault, standing before him covered with his love.**

☐ 42 _____

I have not yet reached my goal, and I am not perfect. But Christ has taken hold of me. So I keep on
running and struggling to take hold of the prize. . . .
I forget what is behind, and I struggle for what is
ahead. I run toward the goal, so that I can win the
prize of being called to heaven. . . . This is the prize
that God offers because of what Christ Jesus has

done. . . . We must keep going in the direction that we are now headed. (Philippians 3:12-14, 16, CEV)

TAKEAWAY
Christ has taken hold of me, so I forget what is behind and struggle for what is ahead.

POWERTHOUGHT It is the defective oyster that produces the pearls.

Seven

I WORRY ABOUT
GROWING OLD

☐ 43 _____

Light is sweet; it's wonderful to see the sun! When
people live to be very old, let them rejoice in every
day of life. But let them also remember that the
dark days will be many. Everything still to come is
meaningless. ❖ For the LORD is good. His unfailing
love continues forever, and his faithfulness continues to each generation. ❖ The unfailing love of the
LORD never ends! By his mercies we have been kept
from complete destruction. Great is his faithfulness;
his mercies begin afresh each day. (Ecclesiastes
11:7-8; Psalm 100:5; Lamentations 3:22-23)

TAKEAWAY
**His faithfulness goes on and on to each succeed-
ing generation.**

I created you and have cared for you since before
you were born. I will be your God throughout your
lifetime—until your hair is white with age. I made
you, and I will care for you. I will carry you along
and save you. (Isaiah 46:3-4)

TAKEAWAY
I will be your God throughout your lifetime—
until your hair is white with age. I made you, and
I will care for you.

The LORD is like a father to his children, tender and
compassionate to those who fear him. For he understands how weak we are; he knows we are only
dust. Our days on earth are like grass; like wildflowers, we bloom and die. The wind blows, and we are
gone—as though we had never been here. But the
love of the LORD remains forever with those who
fear him. His salvation extends to the children's children of those who are faithful to his covenant, of
those who obey his commandments! ❖ Even when I
walk through the dark valley of death, I will not be
afraid, for you are close beside me. Your rod and
your staff protect and comfort me. (Psalms 103:13-
18; 23:4)

TAKEAWAY
The wind blows, and we are gone—as though we
had never been here. But the love of the Lord
remains forever with those who fear him.

_____

White hair is a crown of glory and is seen most among the godly. ❖ The glory of young men is their strength; of old men, their experience. (Proverbs 16:31; 20:29, TLB)

TAKEAWAY

The evening of a well-spent life brings its lamps with it.—Joseph Joubert

_____

LORD, through all the generations you have been our home! . . . You sweep people away like dreams that disappear or like grass that springs up in the morning. . . . Seventy years are given to us! Some may even reach eighty. But even the best of these years are filled with pain and trouble; soon they disappear, and we are gone. . . . Teach us to make the most of our time, so that we may grow in wisdom. (Psalm 90:1, 5, 10, 12)

TAKEAWAY

Teach the older men to exercise self-control, to be worthy of respect, and to live wisely. They must have strong faith and be filled with love and patience. Similarly, teach the older women to live in a way that is appropriate for someone serving the Lord. They must not go around speaking evil of others and must not be heavy drinkers. Instead, they should teach others what is good. These older women must train the younger women to love their husbands and their children. (Titus 2:2-4)

LORD, you alone are my inheritance, my cup of blessing. You guard all that is mine. ❖ Guard me as the apple of your eye. Hide me in the shadow of your wings. . . . But because I have done what is right, I will see you. When I awake, I will be fully satisfied, for I will see you face to face. ❖ But I am trusting you, O LORD, saying, "You are my God!" My future is in your hands. (Psalms 16:5; 17:8, 15; 31:14-15)

T A K E A W A Y
Guard me as the apple of your eye.

Both young men, and maidens; old men, and children: Let them praise the name of the LORD. (Psalm 148:12-13, KJV)

T A K E A W A Y
Yes, the seasons of life pass quickly, and we fade like flowers, here today, gone tomorrow. But the inheritance that never fades away, the one that lasts forever throughout all ages, is eternal life through Jesus Christ.

POWERTHOUGHT

O Jesus, I have promised
To serve thee to the end;
Be thou forever near me,
My Master and my friend;
I shall not fear the battle

If thou art by our side,
Nor wander from the pathway,
If thou wilt be my guide.

—JOHN E. BODE (1816–1874)

Have you ever noticed that a very large number of
people who contributed to the wisdom and events
of the Bible and the progress of the kingdom of
God throughout history were well along in years?

Eight

I WORRY ABOUT MY PURPOSE IN LIFE: WHY AM I HERE?

☐ 50 _____

What doth the LORD require of thee, but to do justly, and to love mercy, and to walk humbly with thy God? (Micah 6:8, KJV)

> *T A K E A W A Y*
> The entire law is summed up in a single command: "Love your neighbor as yourself."
> (Galatians 5:14, NIV)

☐ 51 _____

Owe no man any thing, but to love one another.
❖ Be ye kind one to another. (Romans 13:8; Ephesians 4:32, KJV)

You will find as you look back upon your life that the moments that stand out, the moments when you have really lived, are the moments when you have done things in a spirit of love. Everything else in all our lives is transitory. But the acts of love which no man knows about, or can ever know about—they never fail [to be lasting].
—Henry Drummond, *The Greatest Thing in the World*

□ 52 _____

Wisdom is the principal thing; therefore get wisdom: and with all thy getting get understanding. ❖ Give therefore thy servant an understanding heart . . . that I may discern between good and bad. (Proverbs 4:7; 1 Kings 3:9, KJV)

T A K E A W A Y
Get wisdom . . . to discern between good and bad.

□ 53 _____

Some people have wandered from the faith by following such foolishness. May God's grace be with you all. ❖ Come back to the LORD and live! ❖ I want you to be merciful; I don't want your sacrifices. I want you to know God; that's more important than burnt offerings. (1 Timothy 6:21; Amos 5:6; Hosea 6:6)

T A K E A W A Y
I want you to know me.—God

What doth the LORD thy God require of thee, but to fear the LORD thy God, to walk in all his ways, and to love him, and to serve the LORD thy God with all thy heart and with all thy soul? (Deuteronomy 10:12, KJV)

TAKEAWAY
Fear God, and keep his commandments: for this is the whole duty of man. (Ecclesiastes 12:13, KJV)

Who may worship in your sanctuary, LORD? Who may enter your presence on your holy hill? Those who lead blameless lives and do what is right, speaking the truth from sincere hearts. Those who refuse to slander others or harm their neighbors or speak evil of their friends. Those who despise persistent sinners, and honor the faithful followers of the LORD and keep their promises even when it hurts. Those who do not charge interest on the money they lend, and who refuse to accept bribes to testify against the innocent. Such people will stand firm forever. (Psalm 15)

TAKEAWAY
Do the Duty which lies nearest thee, which thou knowest to be a Duty! Thy second Duty will already have become clearer.—Thomas Carlyle, *Sartor Resartus*

And so, since God in his mercy has given us this wonderful ministry, we never give up. ❖ With Jesus' help, let us continually offer our sacrifice of praise to God by proclaiming the glory of his name. (2 Corinthians 4:1; Hebrews 13:15)

T A K E A W A Y

Let us continually offer our sacrifice of praise to God by proclaiming the glory of his name.

POWERTHOUGHT

If I can stop one Heart from breaking
I shall not live in vain
If I can ease one Life the Aching
Or cool one Pain,
Or help one fainting Robin
Unto his Nest again—
I shall not live in Vain.

—EMILY DICKINSON,
"If I Can Stop One Heart from Breaking"

Nine

I WORRY ABOUT SO MUCH EVIL AND TURMOIL IN THE WORLD

☐ 57 _____

Help, O LORD, for the godly are fast disappearing! The faithful have vanished from the earth! Neighbors lie to each other, speaking with flattering lips and insincere hearts. May the LORD bring their flattery to an end and silence their proud tongues. They say, "We will lie to our hearts' content. Our lips are our own—who can stop us?" The LORD replies, "I have seen violence done to the helpless, and I have heard the groans of the poor. Now I will rise up to rescue them, as they have longed for me to do." The LORD's promises are pure, like silver refined in a furnace, purified seven times over. (Psalm 12:1-6)

T A K E A W A Y

The triumphing of the wicked is short, and the joy of the hypocrite but for a moment. (Job 20:5, KJV)

☐ 58 _____

The wicked are stringing their bows and setting their arrows in the bowstrings. They shoot from the shadows at those who do right. The foundations of law and order have collapsed. What can the righteous do?" But the LORD is in his holy Temple; the LORD still rules from heaven. He watches everything closely, examining everyone on earth. The LORD examines both the righteous and the wicked. He hates everyone who loves violence. He rains down blazing coals on the wicked, punishing them with burning sulfur and scorching winds. For the LORD is righteous, and he loves justice. Those who do what is right will see his face. (Psalm 11:2-7)

T A K E A W A Y

The LORD is in his holy Temple; the LORD still rules from heaven.

☐ 59 _____

For the LORD watches over the path of the godly, but the path of the wicked leads to destruction. Why do the nations rage? Why do the people waste their time with futile plans? The kings of the earth prepare for battle; the rulers plot together against the LORD and against his anointed one. "Let us break their chains," they cry, "and free ourselves from this slavery." But the one who rules in heaven laughs. The Lord scoffs at them. Then in anger he rebukes them, terrifying them with his fierce fury. (Psalms 1:6–2:5)

T A K E A W A Y
How strange that men should try to outwit God!

☐ 60 _____

The nations of the world are as nothing to him. In his eyes they are less than nothing—mere emptiness and froth. . . . It is God who sits above the circle of the earth. The people below must seem to him like grasshoppers! He is the one who spreads out the heavens like a curtain and makes his tent from them. He judges the great people of the world and brings them all to nothing. They hardly get started, barely taking root, when he blows on them and their work withers. The wind carries them off like straw. ❖ For the LORD is king! He rules all the nations. (Isaiah 40:17, 22-24; Psalm 22:28)

T A K E A W A Y
The LORD is King and rules the nations.

☐ 61 _____

The earth is the LORD's, and everything in it. The world and all its people belong to him. For he laid the earth's foundation on the seas and built it on the ocean depths. Who may climb the mountain of the LORD? Who may stand in his holy place? Only those whose hands and hearts are pure, who do not worship idols and never tell lies. They will receive the LORD's blessing and have right standing with

God their savior. They alone may enter God's presence and worship the God of Israel. Open up, ancient gates! Open up, ancient doors, and let the King of glory enter. Who is the King of glory? The LORD, strong and mighty, the LORD, invincible in battle. Open up, ancient gates! Open up, ancient doors, and let the King of glory enter. Who is the King of glory? The LORD Almighty—he is the King of glory. ❖ Thou, O LORD, shalt endure for ever. (Psalms 24; 102:12, KJV)

TAKEAWAY
Everything in all the world belongs to God.

☐ 62 _____

The LORD is king! Let the nations tremble! He sits on his throne between the cherubim. Let the whole earth quake! The LORD sits in majesty in Jerusalem, supreme above all the nations. Let them praise your great and awesome name. Your name is holy! Mighty king, lover of justice, you have established fairness. You have acted with justice and righteousness throughout Israel. ❖ He existed before everything else began, and he holds all creation together. ❖ He has made us his kingdom and his priests who serve before God his Father. Give to him everlasting glory! He rules forever and ever! Amen! (Psalm 99:1-4; Colossians 1:17; Revelation 1:6)

TAKEAWAY
The mighty King Jehovah is determined to give justice. He rules! Amen and Amen!

This is what the LORD says: "Heaven is my throne, and the earth is my footstool. . . . I will bless those who have humble and contrite hearts, who tremble at my word. But those who choose their own ways, delighting in their sins, are cursed. ❖ [The mouths of the wicked] are full of cursing, lies, and threats. Trouble and evil are on the tips of their tongues. They lurk in dark alleys, murdering the innocent who pass by. They are always searching for some helpless victim. Like lions they crouch silently, waiting to pounce on the helpless. Like hunters they capture their victims and drag them away in nets. The helpless are overwhelmed and collapse; they fall beneath the strength of the wicked. The wicked say to themselves, "God isn't watching! He will never notice!" Arise, O LORD! Punish the wicked, O God! Do not forget the helpless! (Isaiah 66:1-3; Psalm 10:7-12)

TAKEAWAY
The LORD is King forever and ever.

POWERTHOUGHT The eyes of the LORD are in every place, beholding the evil and the good. ❖ Now, all glory to God, who is able to keep you from stumbling, and who will bring you into his glorious presence innocent of sin and with great joy. All glory to him, who alone is God our Savior, through Jesus Christ our Lord. Yes, glory, majesty, power, and authority belong to him, in the beginning, now, and forevermore. Amen.—Proverbs 15:3, KJV; Jude 1:24-25

Ten

I WORRY ABOUT MY LOVED ONES: PRAYING THE SCRIPTURES FOR THOSE I LOVE

☐ 64 _____

Our Father which art in heaven, . . . lead us not into temptation, but deliver us from evil. (Matthew 6:9, 13, KJV)

M Y   P R A Y E R :
   Father in heaven, keep all temptation and evil away
   from _____ . If it comes, give_____
   the strength to turn away.
   (Fill in the blanks with your loved one's name.)

☐ 65 _____

May the Lord make you increase and abound in love for one another and for all, just as we abound in love for you. And may he so strengthen your hearts in holiness that you may be blameless before our God. (1 Thessalonians 3:12-13, NRSV)

M Y   P R A Y E R :
I pray that _____ will increase in love for
all people and in holiness so that (s)he might
remain blameless before you, O God.

☐ 66 _____

Make me to know your ways, O LORD; teach me
your paths. Lead me in your truth. ❖ Wondrously
show your steadfast love. . . . Guard me as the apple
of the eye. (Psalms 25:4-5; 17:7-8, NRSV)

M Y   P R A Y E R :
Lord, make _____ a person who reads your
Word. Teach _____ your paths. Encircle
_____ with your steadfast love and guard
_____ as the apple of your eye.

☐ 67 _____

When Jesus had finished saying all these things, he
looked up to heaven and said, "Father, the time has
come. Glorify your Son so he can give glory back
to you. . . . Now I am departing the world; I am leav-
ing them behind and coming to you. Holy Father,
keep them and care for them—all those you have
given me—so that they will be united just as we
are. . . . I'm not asking you to take them out of the
world, but to keep them safe from the evil one. . . .
Make them pure and holy by teaching them your
words of truth." (John 17:1, 11, 15, 17)

M Y   P R A Y E R :
Father, keep _____ in your care. Keep
_____ safe from Satan's power. Make

41

_____ a holy person who reads and abides
by your words of truth in Scripture.

☐ 68 _____

Let every man be swift to hear, slow to speak, slow
to wrath. ❖ Let the words of my mouth, and the
meditation of my heart, be acceptable in thy sight,
O LORD, my strength, and my redeemer. (James
1:19; Psalm 19:14, KJV)

MY PRAYER:

Lord, teach _____ to be a good listener,
someone who thinks before speaking, slow to get
angry. May the thoughts that come in _____'s
mind and the words that _____ speaks be
honoring to you and acceptable in your sight.

☐ 69 _____

May you receive more and more of God's mercy,
peace, and love. ❖ For we are God's masterpiece.
He has created us anew in Christ Jesus, so that we
can do the good things he planned for us long ago.
(Jude 1:2; Ephesians 2:10)

MY PRAYER:

Heavenly Father, heap your kindness and peace
and love upon _____ . Show _____
clearly that it is you who has made us and remade
us in Christ, and that your purpose in pacing us
here on earth is to love and help others. May
_____ satisfy that purpose.

The salvation of the righteous is from the LORD; He is their strength in the time of trouble. And the LORD shall help them and deliver them; He shall deliver them from the wicked, and save them, because they trust in Him. (Psalm 37:39-40, NKJV)

M Y   P R A Y E R :
Lord, teach _____ that you are a strong place to go in times of trouble. May _____ learn early that you have the power to help when problems arise. Teach _____ to trust you and to claim your promises when trouble comes.

POWERTHOUGHT O LORD my God, you are very great; you are clothed with splendor and majesty. . . . He makes the clouds his chariot and rides on the wings of the wind. . . . He set the earth on its foundations; it can never be moved. You covered it with the deep as with a garment; the waters stood above the mountains. . . . They went down into the valleys, to the place you assigned for them. You set a boundary they cannot cross.—Psalm 104:1-9, NIV

M Y   P R A Y E R :
Lord, may _____ learn early about your awesome greatness and power and majesty. May _____ worship you and trust you because you have authority over everything in heaven and earth. May _____ take great joy and comfort in being a child of the King of kings and Lord of lords, Creator of heaven and earth.

Eleven

I WORRY:
I FEEL SO RESTLESS,
SO UNFULFILLED

☐ 71 _____

Everything is so weary and tiresome! No matter how much we see, we are never satisfied. No matter how much we hear, we are not content. ❖ LORD, you will grant us peace, for all we have accomplished is really from you. ❖ Come unto me, all ye that labour and are heavy laden, and I will give you rest. ❖ Peace I leave with you, my peace I give unto you: not as the world giveth, give I unto you. (Ecclesiastes 1:8; Isaiah 26:12; Matthew 11:28; John 14:27, KJV)

T A K E A W A Y
Thou hast made us for thyself, O God, and our hearts are restless until they find their rest in thee.—St. Augustine, *Confessions*

[The "Preacher" said,] "I also tried to find meaning by building huge homes for myself and by planting beautiful vineyards. I made gardens and parks, filling them with all kinds of fruit trees. I built reservoirs to collect the water to irrigate my many flourishing groves. I bought slaves, both men and women, and others were born into my household. I also owned great herds and flocks, more than any of the kings who lived in Jerusalem before me. I collected great sums of silver and gold, the treasure of many kings and provinces. I hired wonderful singers, both men and women, and had many beautiful concubines. I had everything a man could desire! . . . Anything I wanted, I took. I did not restrain myself from any joy. I even found great pleasure in hard work, an additional reward for all my labors. But as I looked at everything I had worked so hard to accomplish, it was all so meaningless. It was like chasing the wind. There was nothing really worthwhile anywhere." (Ecclesiastes 2:4-8, 10-11)

T A K E A W A Y
There is a God-shaped vacuum in the heart of every man which only God can fill through his Son, Jesus Christ.—Blaise Pascal, French philosopher

Just as Death and Destruction are never satisfied, so human desire is never satisfied. ❖ Never let loyalty and kindness get away from you! Wear them like a necklace; write them deep within your heart. Then you will find favor with both God and people, and you will gain a good reputation. Trust in the LORD with all your heart; do not depend on your own understanding. Seek his will in all you do, and he will direct your paths. ❖ *A good prayer to pray:* Turn my eyes from looking at vanities; and give me life in thy ways. (Proverbs 27:20; 3:3-6; Psalm 119:37, RSV)

> *TAKEAWAY*
> **God designed the human machine to run on Himself.—C. S. Lewis**

☐ 74 _____

There is an emptiness at our core that is like a black hole. . . . There is an emptiness in us which threatens to suck us down as well, although what it is actually doing is dispelling an illusion. It is not destroying us, but revealing to us that we are already a dead thing trying to give itself life by taking all within its reach. But the core of us remains an emptiness.—DIOGENES ALLEN, Princeton Seminary professor

> *TAKEAWAY*
> **You will keep in perfect peace all who trust in you, whose thoughts are fixed on you! ❖ But because I have done what is right, I will see you. When I awake, I will be fully satisfied, for I will see you face to face. (Isaiah 26:3; Psalm 17:15)**

☐ 75 _____

We have grasped the mystery of the atom and rejected the Sermon on the Mount.—GEN. OMAR BRADLEY, in 1948

Our hearts are restless till they find their rest in God.

☐ 76 _____

Divine love is perfect peace and joy, it is a freedom from all disquiet, it is all content and happiness and makes everything to rejoice in itself. Love is the Christ of God. Through all the universe of things, nothing is uneasy, unsatisfied, or restless, but because it is not governed by love, or because its nature has not reached or attained the full birth of the spirit of love. For when that is done, every hunger is satisfied, and all complaining, murmuring, accusing, resenting, revenging, and striving are as totally suppressed and overcome, as the coldness, thickness, and horror of darkness are suppressed and overcome by the breaking forth of the light.
—WILLIAM LAW (1686–1761)

T A K E A W A Y
God is love.

☐ 77 _____

So you have everything when you have Christ, and you are filled with God through your union with Christ: ❖ O taste and see that the LORD is good! ❖ Let your roots grow down into [Christ] and draw up nourishment from him, so you will grow in faith, strong and vigorous in the truth you were taught. Let your lives overflow with thanksgiving for all he has done. Don't let anyone lead you astray with empty philosophy and high-sounding nonsense that come from human thinking and from the evil powers of this world, and not from Christ. For in Christ the fullness of God lives in a human body, and you are complete through your union with Christ. He is the Lord over every ruler and authority in the universe. (Psalm 34:8, KJV; Colossians 2:7-10)

> *T A K E A W A Y*
> I have been driven many times to my knees by the overwhelming conviction that I had nowhere else to go. My own wisdom, and that of all about me, seemed insufficient for the day.—Abraham Lincoln

POWERTHOUGHT Contentment is not the fulfillment of what you want but the realization of how much you already have. ❖ You are complete through your union with Christ.—Colossians 2:10

Twelve

I WORRY:
I HAVE TOO MUCH
TO DO

☐ 78 _____

I have observed something else in this world of ours. The fastest runner doesn't always win the race, and the strongest warrior doesn't always win the battle. (Ecclesiastes 9:11)

> *TAKEAWAY*
> **It has been said that what you have become is the price you pay for things you used to want.**

☐ 79 _____

Unless the LORD builds a house, the work of the builders is useless. Unless the LORD protects a city, guarding it with sentries will do no good. It is useless for you to work so hard from early morning until late at night, anxiously working for food to eat; for God gives rest to his loved ones. (Psalm 127:1-2)

My zeal hath consumed me. (Psalm 119:139, KJV)

☐ 80 _____

There is a time for everything, a season for every activity under heaven. A time to be born and a time to die. A time to plant and a time to harvest. A time to kill and a time to heal. A time to tear down and a time to rebuild. A time to cry and a time to laugh. A time to grieve and a time to dance. A time to scatter stones and a time to gather stones. A time to embrace and a time to turn away. A time to search and a time to lose. A time to keep and a time to throw away. A time to tear and a time to mend. A time to be quiet and a time to speak up. A time to love and a time to hate. A time for war and a time for peace. ❖ God has made everything beautiful for its own time. He has planted eternity in the human heart, but even so, people cannot see the whole scope of God's work from beginning to end. (Ecclesiastes 3:1-8, 11)

Where do you want to go in life? How do you want to get there? Do the roles you fill contribute to your goal? What is really important that you do? What merely fills up time? In determining your best roles, keep those that advance you toward your goal and eliminate those that are use-

less and a drag. Your trouble may be too many roles. You cannot afford to take on more than you can handle well.—Henry R. Brandt

☐ 81 _____

My whole lifetime is but a moment to you [O, God]. Proud man! Frail as breath! A shadow! And all his busy rushing ends in nothing. He heaps up riches for someone else to spend. ❖ The love of money is the first step toward all kinds of sin. ❖ What is a man profited, if he shall gain the whole world, and lose his own soul? ❖ Remember your Creator now while you are young—before the silver cord of life snaps and the golden bowl is broken; before the pitcher is broken at the fountain and the wheel is broken at the cistern. (Psalm 39:5-7; 1 Timothy 6:10, TLB; Matthew 16:26, KJV; Ecclesiastes 12:6, TLB)

T A K E A W A Y
Remember your Creator amidst all the turmoil in life.

> *I need Thee ev'ry hour,*
> *Most gracious Lord;*
> *No tender voice like Thine*
> *Can peace afford.*

> —ANNIE S. HAWKS
>   *(1835–1918),*
> *"I Need Thee Ev'ry Hour"*

☐ 82 _____

Cast thy burden upon the LORD, and he shall sustain thee. ❖ Not that we are sufficient of ourselves to think any thing as of ourselves; but our sufficiency is of God. ❖ My grace is sufficient for thee: for my strength is made perfect in weakness. (Psalm 55:22; 2 Corinthians 3:5; 12:9, KJV)

TAKEAWAY
Let the weak say, I am strong. ❖ The LORD will give strength unto his people; the LORD will bless his people with peace. (Joel 3:10; Psalm 29:11, KJV)

☐ 83 _____

In quietness and in confidence shall be your strength. ❖ [Jesus praying to the heavenly Father in our behalf said,] "I'm not asking you to take them out of the world, but to keep them safe from the evil one. They are not part of this world any more than I am. Make them pure and holy by teaching them your words of truth. . . . I am praying not only for these disciples but also for all who will ever believe in me because of their testimony." ❖ So I advise you to live according to your new life in the Holy Spirit. Then you won't be doing what your sinful nature craves. The old sinful nature loves to do evil, which is just opposite from what the Holy Spirit wants. And the Spirit gives us desires that are opposite from what the sinful nature desires. These two forces are constantly fighting each other, and your choices are never free from this conflict. But when you are directed by the Holy Spirit, you are no longer subject to the law. . . . If we are living now by the Holy Spirit, let us follow the Holy Spirit's leading in every part of our lives. (Isaiah 30:15, KJV; John 17:15-17, 20; Galatians 5:16-18, 25)

My workaholic friend struggling with health problems says that each time his mind feels pressured and restless from the day's busyness, he redirects it toward the Lord, dwelling on God's presence and power and majesty. It is his personal form of meditation that stops everything and gets him quiet for a short while. Just what the doctor ordered!

☐ 84 _____

A good prayer for the person who has too much to do: Thou art God. . . . A thousand years in thy sight are but as yesterday when it is past, and as a watch in the night. . . . So teach us to number our days, that we may apply our hearts unto wisdom. . . . Establish thou the work of our hands. (Psalm 90:2, 4, 12, 17, KJV)

T A K E A W A Y
Teach us to number our days, that we may apply our hearts to wisdom.

POWERTHOUGHT Eleanor Roosevelt is said to have carried this prayer in her purse: "Our Father, who has set a restlessness in our hearts and made us all seekers after that which we can never fully find . . . keep us at tasks too hard for us, that we may be driven to Thee for strength." ❖ He giveth power to the faint; and to them that have no might he increaseth strength. ❖ I can do all things through Christ which strengtheneth me. —Isaiah 40:29; Philippians 4:13, KJV

Thirteen

I WORRY:
CAN I COME BACK
TO GOD? HOW?

☐ 85 _____

[Jesus said,] "Those the Father has given me will
come to me, and I will never reject them. . . . And
this is the will of God, that I should not lose even
one of all those he has given me, but that I should
raise them to eternal life at the last day. For it is my
Father's will that all who see his Son and believe in
him should have eternal life—that I should raise
them at the last day." (John 6:37, 39-40)

TAKEAWAY
**Come to Me. . . . The one who comes to Me I
will certainly not cast out.**—Jesus, in John 6:37,
NASB

☐ 86 _____

Ye shall seek me, and find me, when ye shall search
for me with all your heart. ❖ The LORD is good and

54

does what is right; he shows the proper path to those who go astray. (Jeremiah 29:13, KJV; Psalm 25:8)

TAKEAWAY
God's fingers can touch nothing but to mold it into loveliness.—George Macdonald

☐ 87 _____

Voices are heard high on the windswept mountains, the weeping and pleading of Israel's people. For they have forgotten the LORD their God and wandered far from his ways. "My wayward children," says the LORD, "come back to me, and I will heal your wayward hearts." "Yes, we will come," the people reply, "for you are the LORD our God." ❖ "Come now, let us argue this out," says the LORD. "No matter how deep the stain of your sins, I can remove it. I can make you as clean as freshly fallen snow. Even if you are stained as red as crimson, I can make you as white as wool." ❖ I have swept away your sins like the morning mists. I have scattered your offenses like the clouds. Oh, return to me, for I have paid the price to set you free." ❖ To all who mourn in Israel, he will give beauty for ashes, joy instead of mourning, praise instead of despair. For the LORD has planted them like strong and graceful oaks for his own glory. ❖ Let all the godly confess their rebellion to you while there is time, that they may not drown in the floodwaters of judgment. (Jeremiah 3:21-22; Isaiah 1:18; 44:22; 61:3; Psalm 32:6)

TAKEAWAY
You, LORD, have never forsaken those who seek you. (Psalm 9:10, NIV)

Once you were dead, doomed forever because of your many sins. You used to live just like the rest of the world, full of sin, obeying Satan, the mighty prince of the power of the air. He is the spirit at work in the hearts of those who refuse to obey God. All of us used to live that way, following the passions and desires of our evil nature. We were born with an evil nature, and we were under God's anger just like everyone else. But God is so rich in mercy, and he loved us so very much, that even while we were dead because of our sins, he gave us life when he raised Christ from the dead. (It is only by God's special favor that you have been saved!) For he raised us from the dead along with Christ, and we are seated with him in the heavenly realms—all because we are one with Christ Jesus. (Ephesians 2:1-6)

TAKEAWAY

We started out bad, being born with an evil nature. But God loved us so much that he gave us back our lives again.

Remember this—the wrong desires that come into your life aren't anything new and different. Many others have faced exactly the same problems before you. And no temptation is irresistible. ❖ Jesus the Son of God is our great High Priest. . . . This High Priest of ours understands our weaknesses since he had the same temptations we do, though he never once gave way to them and sinned. So let us come boldly to the very throne of God and stay there to receive his mercy and to find grace to help us in our times of need. ❖ A man who refuses to admit his mistakes can never be successful. But if he confesses and forsakes them, he gets another chance. (1 Corinthians 10:13; Hebrews 4:14-16; Proverbs 28:13, TLB)

> *TAKEAWAY*
> A man who refuses to admit his mistakes can never be successful. But if he confesses and forsakes them, he gets another chance.

☐ 90 _____

We all, like sheep, have gone astray, each of us has turned to his own way; and the LORD has laid on him the iniquity of us all. ❖ And having chosen them, he called them to come to him. And he gave them right standing with himself, and he promised them his glory. ❖ Those who become Christians become new persons. They are not the same anymore, for the old life is gone. A new life has begun! (Isaiah 53:6, NIV; Romans 8:30; 2 Corinthians 5:17)

> *TAKEAWAY*
> When we come back to him, he declares us "not guilty" and gives us right standing with himself.

☐ 91 _____

I love them that love me; and those that seek me early shall find me. ❖ Come unto me, all ye that labour and are heavy laden, and I will give you rest. ❖ Only in returning to me and waiting for me will you be saved. ❖ Yet now God declares us "not guilty" of offending him if we trust in Jesus Christ, who in his kindness freely takes away our sins. (Proverbs 8:17; Matthew 11:28, KJV; Isaiah 30:15; Romans 3:24, TLB)

T A K E A W A Y
Come unto me, all ye that labour and are heavy laden, and I will give you rest.

POWERTHOUGHT Brothers! Listen! In this man Jesus there is forgiveness for your sins! Everyone who trusts in him is freed from all guilt and declared righteous.—Acts 13:38-39, TLB

Fourteen

I WORRY:
I NEED HELP WITH
A BAD HABIT

□ 92 _____

Those who become Christians become new persons. They are not the same anymore, for the old life is gone. A new life has begun! ❖ Don't you know that your body is the temple of the Holy Spirit, who lives in you and was given to you by God? You do not belong to yourself, for God bought you with a high price. So you must honor God with your body. ❖ The Holy Spirit helps us in our distress. For we don't even know what we should pray for, nor how we should pray. But the Holy Spirit prays for us with groanings that cannot be expressed in words. (2 Corinthians 5:17; 1 Corinthians 6:19-20; Romans 8:26)

TAKEAWAY
The Holy Spirit helps us in our distress.

Strange as it seems, we Christians actually do have within us a portion of the very thoughts and mind of Christ. ❖ As the Spirit of the Lord works within us, we become more and more like him. (1 Corinthians 2:16; 2 Corinthians 3:18, TLB)

TAKEAWAY

Willpower does not change men. Time does not change men. Christ does. We must go to the source and change the inmost nature, and the angry humors will die away of themselves. Souls are made sweet not by taking the acid fluids out but by putting something in—a great love, a new spirit, the Spirit of Christ.—Henry Drummond, *The Greatest Thing in the World*

Scripture Prayer for Help: My eyes are always looking to the LORD for help, for he alone can rescue me from the traps of my enemies. Turn to me and have mercy on me, for I am alone and in deep distress. My problems go from bad to worse. Oh, save me from them all! Feel my pain and see my trouble. Forgive all my sins. . . . May integrity and honesty protect me, for I put my hope in you. ❖ For he will conceal me there when troubles come; he will hide me in his sanctuary. He will place me out of reach on a high rock. ❖ Save your people! Bless Israel, your special possession! Lead them like a shepherd, and carry them forever in your arms. (Psalms 25:15-18, 21; 27:5; 28:9)

The effective prayer of a righteous man can accomplish much. (James 5:16, NASB)

☐ 95 _____

You were buried with Christ when you were baptized. And with him you were raised to a new life because you trusted the mighty power of God, who raised Christ from the dead. You were dead because of your sins and because your sinful nature was not yet cut away. Then God made you alive with Christ. He forgave all our sins. ❖ Now, all glory to God, who is able to keep you from stumbling, and who will bring you into his glorious presence innocent of sin and with great joy. All glory to him, who alone is God our Savior, through Jesus Christ our Lord. Yes, glory, majesty, power, and authority belong to him, in the beginning, now, and forevermore. Amen. (Colossians 2:12-13; Jude 1:24-25)

TAKEAWAY
As by a Carpenter the world was made, only by that Carpenter can mankind be remade.—Desiderius Erasmus

☐ 96 _____

Scripture Prayer for Help: How can I ever know what sins are lurking in my heart? Cleanse me from these hidden faults. And keep me from deliberate wrongs; help me to stop doing them. . . . May my spoken words and unspoken thoughts be pleasing even to you, O Lord my Rock and my Redeemer. (Psalm 19:12-14, TLB)

☐ 97 _____

[During a time of trouble, the apostle Paul said,] "I don't understand myself at all, for I really want to do what is right, but I don't do it. Instead, I do the very thing I hate. I know perfectly well that what I am doing is wrong, and my bad conscience shows that I agree that the law is good. But I can't help myself, because it is sin inside me that makes me do these evil things. . . . I love God's law with all my heart. But there is another law at work within me that is at war with my mind. . . . Who will free me from this life that is dominated by sin? Thank God! The answer is in Jesus Christ our Lord. So you see how it is: In my mind I really want to obey God's law, but because of my sinful nature I am a slave to sin." ❖ [Jesus said,] "To this end was I born, and for this cause came I into the world, that I should bear witness unto the truth." ❖ Ye shall know the truth, and the truth shall make you free. ❖ I, the LORD, have called you in righteousness; I will take hold of your hand. I will keep you. (Romans 7:15-17, 22-25; John 18:37; 8:32, KJV; Isaiah 42:6, NIV)

T A K E A W A Y
I have learned to place myself before God every day as a vessel to be filled with his Holy Spirit. He has filled me with the blessed assurance that he, as the everlasting God, has guaranteed his own work in me.—Andrew Murray

God rescued Lot out of Sodom because he was a good man who was sick of all the immorality and wickedness around him. Yes, he was a righteous man who was distressed by the wickedness he saw and heard day after day. So you see, the Lord knows how to rescue godly people from their trials, even while punishing the wicked right up until the day of judgment. (2 Peter 2:7-9)

T A K E A W A Y

Faithful is He who calls you, and He also will bring it to pass. (1 Thessalonians 5:24, NASB)

POWERTHOUGHT Resist the devil and he will flee from you. . . . Humble yourselves in the presence of the Lord, and He will exalt you. ❖ Then you will call, and the LORD will answer; you will cry, and He will say, "Here I am." ❖ The angel of the LORD guards all who fear him, and he rescues them. Taste and see that the LORD is good. Oh, the joys of those who trust in him!—James 4:7, 10; Isaiah 58:9, NASB; Psalm 34:7-8

Fifteen

I WORRY:
I HATE SOMEONE

☐ 99 _____

Watch out that no bitterness takes root among you,
for as it springs up it causes deep trouble, hurting
many in their spiritual lives. ❖ You shall not go
about as a slanderer among your people. . . . You
shall not take vengeance, nor bear any grudge, . . .
but you shall love your neighbor as yourself; I am
the LORD. (Hebrews 12:15, TLB; Leviticus 19:16, 18,
NASB)

TAKEAWAY
I am the Lord. Love your neighbor!

☐ 100 _____

People are unreasonable, illogical, and self-centered.
Love them anyway.

If you do good, people will accuse you of selfish, ulterior motives.
  Love them anyway.
The good you do will be forgotten tomorrow.
  Do good anyway.
Honesty and frankness make you vulnerable.
  Be honest and frank anyway.
People really need help but may attack you if you help them.
  Help people anyway.
Give the world the best you have and you'll get kicked in the teeth.
  Give the world the best you've got anyway.
    —FROM A SIGN ON THE WALL OF SHISU BHAVAN, A CALCUTTA
      CHILDREN'S HOME SUPPORTED BY THE EFFORTS OF
                MOTHER TERESA

TAKEAWAY
Love anyway.

☐ 101 _____

Stop judging others, and you will not be judged. For others will treat you as you treat them. Whatever measure you use in judging others, it will be used to measure how you are judged. And why worry about a speck in your friend's eye when you have a log in your own? How can you think of saying, 'Let me help you get rid of that speck in your eye,' when you can't see past the log in your own eye? Hypocrite! First get rid of the log from your own eye; then perhaps you will see well enough to deal with the speck in your friend's eye. (Matthew 7:1-5)

Hate is a prolonged form of suicide.—Douglas V.
Steere, *Dimensions of Prayer*

☐ 102 _____

Don't copy the behavior and customs of this world,
but be a new and different person with a fresh new-
ness in all you do and think. Then you will learn
from your own experience how his ways really satisfy you. ❖ If thine enemy be hungry, give him
bread to eat; and if he be thirsty, give him water to
drink. (Romans 12:2, TLB; Proverbs 25:21, KJV)

TAKEAWAY
He that saith he is in the light, and hateth his
brother, is in darkness. (1 John 2:9, KJV)

☐ 103 _____

You are the salt of the earth. But what good is salt if
it has lost its flavor? Can you make it useful again?
It will be thrown out and trampled underfoot as
worthless. ❖ You must make allowance for each
other's faults and forgive the person who offends
you. Remember, the Lord forgave you, so you must
forgive others. (Matthew 5:13; Colossians 3:13)

TAKEAWAY
Forgive us our debts, as we forgive our debtors.
—Jesus, in Matthew 6:12, KJV

☐ 104 _____

You, Lord, are good, and ready to forgive, and abundant in mercy to all those who call upon You. ❖

[God] is gracious and merciful, slow to anger, and of great kindness; and He relents from doing harm. ❖ He does not treat us as our sins deserve or repay us according to our iniquities. (Psalm 86:5; Joel 2:13, NKJV; Psalm 103:10, NIV)

T A K E A W A Y
He that returns a good for evil obtains the victory.—Thomas Fuller (1608–1661)

☐ 105 _____

If you, O LORD, kept a record of sins, O Lord, who could stand? But with you there is forgiveness. (Psalm 130:3-4, NIV)

T A K E A W A Y
I will forgive their iniquity, and I will remember their sin no more. (Jeremiah 31:34, KJV)

POWERTHOUGHT

Strong hands to weak, old
   hands to young, around the
Christmas board, touch hands.
The false forget, the foe forgive,
   for every guest will go and
   every fire burn low and cabin empty stand.
Forget, forgive, for who may say
   that Christmas day may ever
   come to host or guest again.
Touch hands!

—JOHN NORTON, *Vagabond*

Sixteen

I WORRY:
I CAN'T FORGIVE
SOMEONE

☐ 106 _____

If someone says, "I love God," but hates a Christian
brother or sister, that person is a liar; for if we don't
love people we can see, how can we love God,
whom we have not seen? And God himself has commanded that we must love not only him but our
Christian brothers and sisters, too. (1 John 4:20-21)

TAKEAWAY
**Every person should have a special cemetery lot
in which to bury the faults of friends and loved
ones.**

☐ 107 _____

"In your anger do not sin": Do not let the sun go
down while you are still angry, and do not give the

devil a foothold. . . . Get rid of all bitterness, rage and anger, brawling and slander, along with every form of malice. ❖ Your heavenly Father will forgive you if you forgive those who sin against you; but if *you* refuse to forgive *them, he* will not forgive *you*. (Ephesians 4:26-27, 31, NIV; Matthew 6:14-15, TLB)

TAKEAWAY

When we hate our enemies, we give them power over us—power over our sleep, our appetites, our blood pressure, our health, and our happiness. Our enemies would dance with joy if they surmised that they worry and lacerate us. Our hatred is not hurting them at all; it only turns our own days and nights into a hellish turmoil.—Author Unknown

□ 108 _____

Put off your old self, which is being corrupted by its deceitful desires; to be made new in the attitude of your [mind]. ❖ If you love only those who love you, what good is that? Even scoundrels do that much. If you are friendly only to your friends, how are you different from anyone else? Even the heathen do that. ❖ Bless them which persecute you: bless, and curse not. (Ephesians 4:22-23, NIV; Matthew 5:46-47, TLB; Romans 12:14, KJV)

TAKEAWAY

If we could read the secret history of our enemies, we should find in each man sorrow and suffering enough to disarm all hostility.—Henry Wadsworth Longfellow, *Driftwood*

The merciful man doeth good to his own soul. He that despiseth his neighbour sinneth. (Proverbs 11:17; 14:21, KJV)

> TAKEAWAY
> **Father, forgive them; for they know not what they do.**—Jesus, speaking from the cross in Luke 23:34, KJV

People with hate in their hearts may sound pleasant enough, but don't believe them. Though they pretend to be kind, their hearts are full of all kinds of evil. While their hatred may be concealed by trickery, it will finally come to light for all to see. (Proverbs 26:24-26)

> TAKEAWAY
> **It is better that my enemy see good in me than that I see bad in him.**—Ancient Proverb

Ye have heard that it hath been said, Thou shalt love thy neighbour, and hate thine enemy. But I say unto you, Love your enemies, bless them that curse you, do good to them that hate you, and pray for them which despitefully use you, and persecute you; that ye may be the children of your Father which is in heaven: for he maketh his sun to rise on the evil and on the good, and sendeth rain on the just and on the unjust. (Matthew 5:43-45, KJV)

He maketh his sun to rise on the evil and on the good, and sendeth rain on the just and on the unjust. (Matthew 5:45, KJV)

☐ 112 _____

Peter came to [Jesus] and asked, "Lord, how often should I forgive someone who sins against me? Seven times?" "No!" Jesus replied, "seventy times seven!" (Matthew 18:21-22)

T A K E A W A Y
To forgive is to set a prisoner free and discover the prisoner was *you!*

POWERTHOUGHT The rose keeps on giving its fragrance even when thrown into the trash. ❖ My resolve: I will keep on loving anyway, even when "trashed" by somebody else.

Seventeen

I WORRY: DOES GOD REALLY KNOW BEST?

☐ 113 _____

The wisdom that comes from heaven is first of all pure. It is also peace loving, gentle at all times, and willing to yield to others. It is full of mercy and good deeds. It shows no partiality and is always sincere. ❖ "For I know the plans I have for you," says the LORD. "They are plans for good and not for disaster, to give you a future and a hope. ❖ I am trusting you, O LORD, saying, "You are my God!" My future is in your hands. (James 3:17; Jeremiah 29:11; Psalm 31:14-15)

TAKEAWAY
God is sovereign; he does not need to ask my permission.

☐ 114 _____

O the depth of the riches both of the wisdom and knowledge of God! how unsearchable are his judg-

ments, and his ways past finding out! ❖ Let [the
Lord] do what seemeth him good. ❖ If it be of God,
ye cannot overthrow [his will]; lest haply ye be
found even to fight against God. (Romans 11:33;
1 Samuel 3:18; Acts 5:39, KJV)

TAKEAWAY
Lord of Lords, grant us the good whether we
pray for it or not, but evil keep from us, even
though we pray for it.—Plato

Have you ever looked back to thank God that all
your prayers that seemed so urgent then have not
been answered yes? Think about it.

☐ 115 _____

Thus saith the LORD . . . I know the things that
come into your mind, every one of them. ❖ My
thoughts are not your thoughts, neither are your
ways my ways, saith the LORD. ❖ The ways of the
LORD are right, and the just shall walk in them. (Ezekiel 11:5; Isaiah 55:8; Hosea 14:9, KJV)

TAKEAWAY
Speak, LORD; for thy servant heareth. (1 Samuel
3:9, KJV)

☐ 116 _____

How deep are [God's] wisdom and knowledge!
Who can explain his decisions? Who can understand his ways? As the scripture says, "Who knows
the mind of the Lord? Who is able to give him
advice? Who has ever given him anything so that

he had to pay it back?" For all things were created by him, and all things exist through him and for him. To God be the glory forever! Amen. (Romans 11:33-36, TEV)

TAKEAWAY
How deep are his wisdom and knowledge!

☐ 117 _____

Shall any teach God knowledge? ❖ He is God in heaven above, and in earth beneath. ❖ [Nebuchadnezzar, after a humbling experience, said:] "All the people of the earth are nothing compared to him. He has the power to do as he pleases among the angels of heaven and with those who live on earth. No one can stop him or challenge him, saying, 'What do you mean by doing these things?' . . . I . . . praise and glorify and honor the King of heaven. All his acts are just and true, and he is able to humble those who are proud." (Job 21:22; Joshua 2:11, KJV; Daniel 4:35, 37)

TAKEAWAY
Let him do to me as seemeth good unto him. (2 Samuel 15:26, KJV)

☐ 118 _____

All glory to him, who alone is God our Savior, through Jesus Christ our Lord. Yes, glory, majesty, power, and authority belong to him, in the beginning, now, and forevermore. ❖ He has showered his kindness on us, along with all wisdom and understanding. ❖ We know that God causes everything to work together for the good of those who love God and are called according to his purpose for them. (Jude 1:25; Ephesians 1:8; Romans 8:28)

TAKEAWAY

This is a wise, sane Christian faith: that a man commit himself, his life and his hopes to God; that God undertakes the special protection of that man; that therefore that man ought not to be afraid of anything!—George Macdonald

☐ 119 ─────────────────────────────

There is a way that seems right to a man, but its end is the way of death. ❖ When [the Israelites in the wilderness] complained [about their food; they were tired of manna], it displeased the LORD. . . . "Who will give us meat to eat? We remember the fish which we ate freely in Egypt, the cucumbers, the melons, the leeks, the onions, and the garlic. . . . Now . . . there is nothing at all except this manna!". . . Now a wind went out from the LORD, and it brought quail from the sea and left them fluttering near the camp. . . . And the people stayed up all that day, all night, and all the next day, and gathered the quail . . . ; and they spread them out for themselves all around the camp. ❖ They did not wait for His counsel, but lusted exceedingly in the wilderness, and tested God in the desert. And He gave them their request, but sent leanness into their soul. (Proverbs 14:12; Numbers 11:1, 4-5, 31-32; Psalm 106:13-15, NKJV)

Not my will, but thine, be done.—Jesus, in Luke 22:42, KJV

POWERTHOUGHT The third clause of the Lord's Prayer (Thy will be done) is repeated daily by millions, who have not the slightest intention of letting any will be done except their own.—ALDOUS HUXLEY, *The Perennial Philosophy*

Eighteen

I WORRY:
SOMETIMES MY FAITH
GROWS WEAK

☐ 120 _____

The fool hath said in his heart, There is no God.
❖ Is the LORD among us, or not? ❖ Thou shalt find
him, if thou seek him with all thy heart and with all
thy soul. ❖ If thou seek him, he will be found of
thee. (Psalm 14:1; Exodus 17:7; Deuteronomy 4:29;
1 Chronicles 28:9, KJV)

TAKEAWAY
Begin to weave and God will give the thread.
—German Proverb

☐ 121 _____

[Blind Bartimaeus cried out,] "Jesus, thou son of
David, have mercy on me." . . . And Jesus said unto
him, "Go thy way; thy faith hath made thee whole."
And immediately he received his sight. ❖ The Jew-

ish leaders surrounded [Jesus] and asked, "How long are you going to keep us in suspense? If you are the Messiah, tell us plainly." Jesus replied, "I have already told you, and you don't believe me. The proof is what I do in the name of my Father. . . . The Father and I are one." ❖ Jesus' disciples saw him do many other miraculous signs besides the ones recorded in this book. But these are written so that you may believe that Jesus is the Messiah, the Son of God, and that by believing in him you will have life. (Mark 10:47, 52, KJV; John 10:24-25, 30; 20:30-31)

TAKEAWAY
These are written so that you may believe that Jesus is the Messiah, the Son of God, and that by believing in him you will have life.

☐ 122 _____

Faith should not stand in the wisdom of men, but in the power of God. ❖ In the beginning God created the heaven and the earth. And the earth was without form, and void; and darkness was upon the face of the deep. And the Spirit of God moved upon the face of the waters. And God said, Let there be light: and there was light. And God saw the light, that it was good: and God divided the light from the darkness. And God called the light Day, and the darkness he called Night. . . . And God said, Let there be lights in the firmament of the heaven to divide the day from the night; and let them be for signs, and for seasons, and for days, and years. . . . And God created great whales, and every living creature that moveth. . . . And God said, Let us make man in our image. (1 Corinthians 2:5; Genesis 1:1-5, 14, 21, 26, KJV)

> TAKEAWAY
> **Faith is a resting of the heart in the sufficiency of the evidences.—Clark H. Pinnock**

Faith is not a feeling!

□ 123 _____

[Thomas said,] Except I shall see in his hands the print of the nails, and put my finger into the print of the nails, and thrust my hand into his side, I will not believe. . . . Then saith [Jesus] to Thomas, Reach hither thy finger, and behold my hands; and reach hither thy hand, and thrust it into my side: and be not faithless, but believing. And Thomas answered and said unto him, My Lord and my God. (John 20:25-28, KJV)

> TAKEAWAY
> **O thou of little faith, wherefore didst thou doubt?—Jesus, in Matthew 14:31, KJV**

□ 124 _____

The Word was made flesh, and dwelt among us (and we beheld his glory, the glory as of the only begotten of the Father), full of grace and truth. ❖ From that time many of [Jesus'] disciples went back, and walked no more with him. Then said Jesus unto the twelve, Will ye also go away? Then Simon Peter answered him, Lord, to whom shall we go? thou hast the words of eternal life. And we believe and are sure that thou art that Christ, the Son of the living God. (John 1:14; 6:66-69 KJV)

TAKEAWAY

I know whom I have believed, and am persuaded that he is able to keep that which I have committed unto him against that day. (The apostle Paul in 2 Timothy 1:12, KJV)

□ 125 _____

I prayed for faith and thought that some day faith would come down and strike me like lightning. But faith did not seem to come. One day I read in the tenth chapter of Romans, "Faith cometh by hearing, and hearing by the Word of God." I had up to this time closed my Bible and prayed for faith. I now opened my Bible and began to study, and faith has been growing ever since.—DWIGHT L. MOODY

TAKEAWAY

Faith rests on the naked Word of God; that Word believed gives full assurance.—H. A. Ironside

Faith comes from hearing, and hearing by the word of Christ. (Romans 10:17, NASB)

□ 126 _____

I arise today
Through God's strength to pilot me:
God's wisdom to guide me,
God's eye to look before me,
God's ear to hear me,
God's word to speak for me,

God's hand to guard me,
God's way to lie before me,
God's shield to protect me.
Christ be with me, Christ before me,
Christ behind me,
Christ in me, Christ beneath me,
Christ above me,
Christ on my right, Christ on my left,
Christ when I lie down, Christ when I sit down,
Christ when I arise,
Christ in the heart of every man who thinks of me,
Christ in the mouth of every one who speaks of me,
Christ in every eye that sees me,
Christ in every ear that hears me.

—St. Patrick, c. 390

T A K E A W A Y
By faith ye stand. (2 Corinthians 1:24, KJV)

POWERTHOUGHT Lord, I believe; help thou mine unbelief.—Mark 9:24, KJV

Nineteen

I WORRY: GOD, YOU SEEM SO FAR AWAY

☐ 127 _____

O LORD, you have examined my heart and know everything about me. You know when I sit down or stand up. You know my every thought when far away. You chart the path ahead of me and tell me where to stop and rest. (Psalm 139:1-3)

TAKEAWAY
You know when I sit or stand. You know my every thought.

☐ 128 _____

No one has ever seen God. But if we love each other, God lives in us, and his love has been brought to full expression through us. And God has given us his Spirit as proof that we live in him and he in us. Furthermore, we have seen with our own eyes and now testify that the Father sent his Son to be the Savior of the world. All who proclaim that Jesus is the Son of God have God living in them, and they live in God. (1 John 4:12-15)

TAKEAWAY
God lives in us.

☐ 129 _____

God is with those who obey him. (Psalm 14:5)

TAKEAWAY
In the pure, strong hours of the morning, when the soul of the day is at its best, lean upon the window sill of God and look into his face, and get the orders for the day. Then go out into the day with the sense of a Hand upon your shoulder and not a chip.—E. Stanley Jones

☐ 130 _____

The LORD is in His holy temple, the LORD's throne is in heaven; His eyes behold, His eyelids test the sons of men. ❖ You shall keep them, O LORD, You shall preserve them from this generation forever. (Psalms 11:4; 12:7, NKJV)

TAKEAWAY
His eyelids test the sons of men.

☐ 131 _____

How long, O LORD? Will you forget me forever? How long will you hide your face from me? How long must I wrestle with my thoughts and every day have sorrow in my heart? How long will my enemy triumph over me? Look on me and answer, O LORD my God. Give light to my eyes, or . . . my enemy will say, "I have overcome him," and my foes will rejoice when I fall. But I trust in your unfailing love; my heart rejoices in your salvation. I will sing to the LORD, for he has been good to me. The fool says in his heart, "There is no God." (Psalms 13:1–14:1, NIV)

TAKEAWAY
Look on me and answer, O LORD my God. . . .
I trust in your unfailing love.

☐ 132 _____

[Jesus said,] "If you love me, obey my commandments. And I will ask the Father, and he will give you another Counselor, who will never leave you. He is the Holy Spirit, who leads into all truth. The world at large cannot receive him, because it isn't looking for him and doesn't recognize him. But you do, because he lives with you now and later will be in you. No, I will not abandon you as orphans—I will come to you." (John 14:15-18)

TAKEAWAY
I will give you another Comforter who will never
leave you.

☐ 133 _____

Arise, LORD! Lift up your hand, O God. Do not forget the helpless. . . . You, O God, do see trouble and grief; you consider it to take it in hand. The victim commits himself to you; you are the helper of the fatherless. . . . You hear, O LORD, the desire of the afflicted; you encourage them, and you listen to their cry . . . in order that man, who is of the earth, may terrify no more. In the LORD I take refuge. (Psalms 10:12, 14, 17–11:1, NIV)

> TAKEAWAY
> You, O God, see trouble and grief and listen to the cry of the afflicted.

POWERTHOUGHT The LORD keeps close watch over the whole world, to give strength to those whose hearts are loyal to him.—2 Chronicles 16:9, TEV

Twenty

I WORRY:
I CAN'T SLEEP

☐ 134 _____

Blessed are all who take refuge in him. ❖ Many are
saying of me, "God will not deliver him." But you
are a shield around me, O LORD; you bestow glory
on me and lift up my head. To the LORD I cry aloud,
and he answers me from his holy hill. I lie down
and sleep; I wake again, because the LORD sustains
me. I will not fear the tens of thousands drawn up
against me on every side. . . . From the LORD comes
deliverance. (Psalms 2:12; 3:2-6, 8, NIV)

> TAKEAWAY
> You are a shield around me, O Lord. I lie down
> and sleep. The Lord sustains me.

☐ 135 _____

When you are on your beds, search your hearts and
be silent. . . . Trust in the LORD. Many are asking,
"Who can show us any good?" Let the light of your
face shine upon us, O LORD. . . . I will lie down and

sleep in peace, for you alone, O LORD, make me
dwell in safety. (Psalm 4:4-8, NIV)

T A K E A W A Y
**With the light of your face shining upon me,
O Lord, I will lie down and sleep in peace.**

☐ 136 _____

The day is yours, and yours also the night; you established the sun and moon. It was you who set all
the boundaries of the earth; you made both summer
and winter. ❖ Keep me safe, O God, for in you I
take refuge. . . . I will praise the LORD, who counsels
me; even at night my heart instructs me. I have set
the LORD always before me. Because he is at my
right hand, I will not be shaken. Therefore my heart
is glad and my tongue rejoices; my body also will
rest secure. (Psalms 74:16-17; 16:1, 7-9, NIV)

T A K E A W A Y
**Because God is at my right hand, my body will
rest secure.**

☐ 137 _____

O God, you are my God, earnestly I seek you; my
soul thirsts for you, my body longs for you, in a dry
and weary land where there is no water. . . . Because
your love is better than life, my lips will glorify you. I
will praise you as long as I live, and in your name I
will lift up my hands. . . . On my bed I remember
you; I think of you through the watches of the night.
Because you are my help, I sing in the shadow of

your wings. My soul clings to you; your right hand upholds me. (Psalm 63:1-8, NIV)

T A K E A W A Y

I think of you through the watches of the night. My soul clings to you.

☐ 138 _____

How precious are your thoughts about me, O God! They are innumerable! I can't even count them; they outnumber the grains of sand! And when I wake up in the morning, you are still with me! (Psalm 139:17-18)

T A K E A W A Y

You are thinking about me constantly. And when I wake in the morning, you are still thinking of me!

☐ 139 _____

My body also will rest secure, because you will not abandon me. . . . You have made known to me the path of life; you will fill me with joy in your presence. ❖ Though you probe my heart and examine me at night, though you test me, you will find nothing. . . . My steps have held to your paths; my feet have not slipped. . . . Keep me as the apple of your eye; hide me in the shadow of your wings. . . . And I—in righteousness I will see your face; when I awake, I will be satisfied with seeing your likeness. I love you, O LORD, my strength. (Psalms 16:9-11; 17:3–18:1, NIV)

Keep me as the apple of your eye. Hide me in the
shadow of your wings. I love you, O Lord, my
strength.

☐ 140 _____

Blessed is the man who does not walk in the counsel
of the wicked or stand in the way of sinners or sit in
the seat of mockers. But his delight is in the law of
the LORD, and on his law he meditates day and
night. He is like a tree planted by streams of water,
which yields its fruit in season and whose leaf does
not wither. Whatever he does prospers. . . . For the
LORD watches over the way of the righteous. (Psalm
1, NIV)

T A K E A W A Y
On your word, O Lord, I meditate day and night.
I am like a tree planted by streams of water.

POWERTHOUGHT

Hidden in the hollow
Of His blessed hand,
Never foe can follow,
Never traitor stand;
Not a surge of worry,
Not a shade of care,
Not a blast of hurry,
Touch the spirit there.

Stayed upon Jehovah
Hearts are fully blest;

Finding as He promised,
Perfect peace and rest.

—FRANCES R. HAVERGAL
(1837–1879)

Twenty-one

I WORRY: WHERE SHALL I GO FOR HELP?

☐ 141 _____

What I want from you is your true thanks; I want
your promises fulfilled. *I want you to trust me in your
times of trouble, so I can rescue you and you can give me
glory.* ❖ Our help is from the LORD who made
heaven and earth. (Psalms 50:14-15; 124:8, TLB)

   T A K E A W A Y
   Our help is from the Lord.

☐ 142 _____

Remember the days of old, consider the years of
many generations: ask thy father, and he will shew
thee; thy elders, and they will tell thee. ❖ He that
walketh with wise men shall be wise. (Deuteronomy 32:7; Proverbs 13:20, KJV)

Ask the elders. He who walks with wise men shall
be wise.

☐ 143 _____

Everything in the Scriptures is God's Word. All of it
is useful for teaching and helping people and for cor-
recting them and showing them how to live. (2 Timothy 3:16, CEV)

T A K E A W A Y
God's Word is useful for helping people and showing them how to live.

☐ 144 _____

This is what the LORD says: "Cursed are those who
put their trust in mere humans and turn their hearts
away from the LORD. They are like stunted shrubs in
the desert, with no hope for the future. They will live
in the barren wilderness, on the salty flats where no
one lives. But blessed are those who trust in the LORD
and have made the LORD their hope and confidence."
. . . But we worship at your throne—eternal, high, and
glorious! ❖ As for me and my family, we will serve the
LORD. (Jeremiah 17:5-7, 12; Joshua 24:15)

T A K E A W A Y
Blessed is the man who has made the Lord his
hope and confidence.

☐ 145 _____

I pray that you will begin to understand the incredible greatness of his power for us who believe him.

This is the same mighty power that raised Christ from the dead and seated him in the place of honor at God's right hand in the heavenly realms. (Ephesians 1:19-20)

TAKEAWAY
How incredibly great is his power to help those who believe!

☐ 146 _____

God is our refuge and strength, an ever-present help in trouble. Therefore we will not fear, though the earth give way and the mountains fall into the heart of the sea, though its waters roar and foam and the mountains quake with their surging. (Psalm 46:1-3, NIV)

TAKEAWAY
God is our refuge and strength, an ever-present help in trouble.

☐ 147 _____

In my distress I called to the LORD; I cried to my God for help. From his temple he heard my voice; my cry came before him, into his ears. The earth trembled and quaked, and the foundations of the mountains shook; they trembled because he was angry. Smoke rose from his nostrils; consuming fire came from his mouth, burning coals blazed out of it. He parted the heavens and came down; dark clouds were under his feet. He mounted the cherubim and flew; he soared on the wings of the wind. . . . He reached down from on high and took hold of me; he drew me out of deep waters. . . . He brought me out into a spacious place; he rescued me because he delighted in me. (Psalm 18:6-19, NIV)

TAKEAWAY
He drew me out of deep waters. . . . He rescued me because he delighted in me.

POWERTHOUGHT The Bible is a book in comparison with which all others in my eyes are of minor importance, and which in all my perplexities and distresses has never failed to give me light and strength.—GEN. ROBERT E. LEE

Twenty-two

I WORRY: CAN I COPE WITH MY PROBLEMS?

☐ 148 _____

The Sovereign LORD is my strength! He will make me as surefooted as a deer and bring me safely over the mountains. ❖ I can do everything with the help of Christ who gives me the strength I need. (Habakkuk 3:19; Philippians 4:13)

> *TAKEAWAY*
> **In Him we live and move and exist, . . . "for we also are His offspring." (Acts 17:28, NASB)**

☐ 149 _____

LORD, how I love you! . . . In your strength I can scale any wall, attack any troop. What a God he is! How perfect in every way! All his promises prove true. He is a shield for everyone who hides behind him. For who is God except our Lord? Who but he is as a rock? He fills me with strength and protects me wherever I go. He gives me the surefootedness of a mountain goat upon the crags. He leads me safely along the top of the cliffs. . . . God is alive! Praise him who is the great rock of protection. (Psalm 18:1, 29-33, 46, TLB)

TAKEAWAY

Cast yourself into the arms of God and be very sure that if He wants anything of you, He will fit you for the work and give you strength.—Philip Neri (1515–1595)

☐ 150 _____

If we are unfaithful, he remains faithful, for he cannot deny himself. (2 Timothy 2:13)

TAKEAWAY

Even when our faith runs out, he remains faithful to us to help us.

☐ 151 _____

May the Lord bring you into an ever deeper understanding of the love of God and the endurance that comes from Christ. ❖ You will keep in perfect peace all who trust in you, whose thoughts are fixed on you! Trust in the LORD always, for the LORD GOD is the eternal Rock. (2 Thessalonians 3:5; Isaiah 26:3-4)

TAKEAWAY

He will keep in perfect peace all who trust in him.

It is not by force nor by strength, but by my Spirit,
says the LORD Almighty. (Zechariah 4:6)

> **TAKEAWAY**
> You will succeed because of my Spirit, not by
> your own might.

I was given a thorn in my flesh, a messenger from
Satan to torment me and keep me from getting proud.
Three different times I begged the Lord to take it
away. Each time he said, "My gracious favor is all you
need. My power works best in your weakness." So
now I am glad to boast about my weaknesses, so that
the power of Christ may work through me. Since I
know it is all for Christ's good, I am quite content
with my weaknesses and with insults, hardships, perse-
cutions, and calamities. For when I am weak, then I
am strong. (2 Corinthians 12:7-10)

> **TAKEAWAY**
> I am with you. That is all you need. My power
> shows up best in weak people.

I am holding you by your right hand—I, the LORD
your God. And I say to you, "Do not be afraid. I am
here to help you." (Isaiah 41:13)

> **TAKEAWAY**
> I am holding you by your right hand. Don't be
> afraid.

POWERTHOUGHT Every step of progress the world has made has been from scaffold to scaffold, and from stake to stake.—WENDELL PHILLIPS

Twenty-three

I WORRY: NOBODY SEEMS TO CARE ABOUT ME

☐ 155 _____

Who shall separate us from the love of Christ? shall tribulation, or distress, or persecution, or famine, or nakedness, or peril, or sword? . . . Nay, in all these things we are more than conquerors through him that loved us. For I am persuaded that neither death, nor life, nor angels, nor principalities, nor powers, nor things present, nor things to come, nor height, nor depth, nor any other creature, shall be able to separate us from the love of God, which is in Christ Jesus our Lord. (Romans 8:35-39, KJV)

TAKEAWAY

I am persuaded that neither death, nor life, nor angels, nor principalities, nor powers, nor things present, nor things to come, or height, nor depth, nor any other creature shall be able to separate us from the love of God.

He will feed his flock like a shepherd. He will carry
the lambs in his arms, holding them close to his
heart. He will gently lead the mother sheep with
their young. (Isaiah 40:11)

> TAKEAWAY
> **He will feed his flock like a shepherd.**

May your roots go down deep into the soil of God's
marvelous love; and may you be able to feel and understand, as all God's children should, how long,
how wide, how deep, and how high his love really
is; and to experience this love for yourselves,
though it is so great that you will never see the end
of it or fully know or understand it. And so at last
you will be filled up with God himself. (Ephesians
3:17-19, TLB)

> TAKEAWAY
> **May your roots go down deep into the soil of
> God's marvelous love.**

All praise to him who always loves us and who set
us free from our sins by pouring out his lifeblood
for us. ❖ In this act we see what real love is. (Revelation 1:5; 1 John 4:10, TLB)

> TAKEAWAY
> **In [Jesus' act of] pouring out his lifeblood for us,
> we see what real love is.**

_____

Not even a sparrow, worth only half a penny, can
fall to the ground without your Father knowing it.
And the very hairs on your head are all numbered.
So don't be afraid; you are more valuable to him
than a whole flock of sparrows. (Matthew 10:29-31)

TAKEAWAY
Don't worry. You are very valuable to him.

☐ 160 _____

See how very much our heavenly Father loves us,
for he allows us to be called his children—think of
it—and we really *are!* But since most people don't
know God, naturally they don't understand that we
are his children. Yes, dear friends, we are already
God's children, right now. ❖ They say, "My Lord
deserted us; he has forgotten us." "Never! Can a
mother forget her little child and not have love for
her own son? Yet even if that should be, I will not
forget you." (1 John 3:1-2; Isaiah 49:14-15, TLB)

TAKEAWAY
**See how much our heavenly Father loves us, for
he allows us to be called his children—think of
it!—and we really *are!***

☐ 161 _____

The LORD your God is with you, he is mighty to
save. He will take great delight in you, he will quiet
you with his love, he will rejoice over you with singing. (Zephaniah 3:17, NIV)

He will quiet you with his love, he will rejoice
over you with singing.

POWERTHOUGHT Didst Thou give me this inescap-
able loneliness so that it would be easier to give Thee all?
—DÄG HAMMARSKJÖLD, *Markings*

Twenty-four

I WORRY:
I CAN'T RELAX
MY MIND

☐ 162 _____

Don't be afraid, for I am with you. Do not be dismayed, for I am your God. I will strengthen you. I will help you. I will uphold you with my victorious right hand. (Isaiah 41:10)

TAKEAWAY
Fear not, for I am with you. I am your God. I will help you.

☐ 163 _____

We can say with confidence, "The Lord is my helper, so I will not be afraid. What can mere mortals do to me?". . . Jesus Christ is the same yesterday, today, and forever. (Hebrews 13:6-8)

TAKEAWAY
The Lord is my helper and I am not afraid of anything that mere man can do to me.

Though he slay me, yet will I trust in him. ❖ Even
though the fig trees have no blossoms, and there
are no grapes on the vine; even though the olive
crop fails, and the fields lie empty and barren; even
though the flocks die in the fields, and the cattle
barns are empty, yet I will rejoice in the LORD! I will
be joyful in the God of my salvation. (Job 13:15,
KJV; Habakkuk 3:17-18)

T A K E A W A Y
Though he slay me, yet will I trust in him.

☐ 165 _____

There is a time for everything, a season for every
activity under heaven. . . . A time to be quiet and a
time to speak up. ❖ The LORD is in his holy Temple.
Let all the earth be silent before him. (Ecclesiastes
3:1, 7; Habakkuk 2:20)

T A K E A W A Y
**Anxiety is the natural result when our hopes are
centered in anything short of God and his will for
us.—Billy Graham**

☐ 166 _____

You are my hiding place; you shall preserve me
from trouble; You shall surround me with songs of
deliverance. . . . Many sorrows shall be to the
wicked; but he who trusts in the LORD, mercy shall
surround him. ❖ The LORD is my rock and my fortress and my deliverer; my God, my strength, in

whom I will trust; my shield and the horn of my salvation, my stronghold. (Psalms 32:7, 10; 18:2, NKJV)

TAKEAWAY

The Lord is my hiding place, my rock, my fortress, my deliverer, my strength, my shield, my stronghold.

□ 167 _____

If God cares so wonderfully for flowers that are here today and gone tomorrow, won't he more surely care for you, O men of little faith? So don't worry at all about having enough food and clothing. Why be like the heathen? For they take pride in all these things and are deeply concerned about them. But your heavenly Father already knows perfectly well that you need them, and he will give them to you if you give him first place in your life and live as he wants you to. (Matthew 6:30-33, TLB)

TAKEAWAY

If God cares so wonderfully for flowers that are here today and gone tomorrow, won't he more surely care for you if you give him first place in your life?

□ 168 _____

Gird up the loins of your mind. ❖ Don't worry about tomorrow, for tomorrow will bring its own worries. Today's trouble is enough for today. (1 Peter 1:13, KJV; Matthew 6:34)

TAKEAWAY

Live one day at a time.

POWERTHOUGHT

Breathe through the heats of our desire
Thy coolness and thy balm;
Let sense be dumb, let flesh retire,
Speak through the earthquake, wind, and fire
O still small voice of calm!

—JOHN GREENLEAF WHITTIER,
"Dear Lord and Father of Mankind"

Twenty-five

I WORRY:
I'M SO WEARY

☐ 169 _____

Have you never heard or understood? Don't you
know that the LORD is the everlasting God, the Creator of all the earth? He never grows faint or weary.
No one can measure the depths of his understanding.
He gives power to those who are tired and worn out;
he offers strength to the weak. Even youths will
become exhausted, and young men will give up. But
those who wait on the LORD will find new strength.
They will fly high on wings like eagles. They will run
and not grow weary. They will walk and not faint.
(Isaiah 40:28-31)

> ### TAKEAWAY
> **God never grows weary. He gives power to the
> tired and worn out, and strength to the weak.**

☐ 170 _____

We never give up. Though our bodies are dying,
our inner strength in the Lord is growing every day.

❖ I am the Lord, the God of all mankind; is there anything too hard for me? (2 Corinthians 4:16; Jeremiah 32:27, TLB)

TAKEAWAY
Though our bodies are dying, our inner strength in the Lord is growing every day.

☐ 171 _____

Because the Lord is my Shepherd, I have everything I need! ❖ In him we live, and move, and have our being. (Psalm 23:1, TLB; Acts 17:28, KJV)

TAKEAWAY
In him I live, and move, and have my being.

☐ 172 _____

Trust in the LORD and do good. Then you will live safely in the land and prosper. Take delight in the LORD, and he will give you your heart's desires. . . . Be still in the presence of the LORD, and wait patiently for him to act. Don't worry about evil people who prosper or fret about their wicked schemes. Stop your anger! Turn from your rage! Do not envy others—it only leads to harm. . . . Those who are gentle and lowly will possess the land; they will live in prosperous security. (Psalm 37:3-4, 7-8, 11)

TAKEAWAY
Commit everything you do to the Lord. Trust him to help you do it and he will. Rest in the Lord.

He is close to all who call on him sincerely. . . . I will praise the Lord and call on all men everywhere to bless his holy name forever and ever. ❖ For since he himself has been through suffering and temptation, he knows what it is like when we suffer and are tempted, and he is wonderfully able to help us. (Psalm 145:18, 21; Hebrews 2:18, TLB)

TAKEAWAY
He is close to all who call on him sincerely.

Here on earth you will have many trials and sorrows. But take heart, because I have overcome the world. (John 16:33)

TAKEAWAY
Take heart, because I have overcome the world.

Therefore, since we are surrounded by such a huge crowd of witnesses to the life of faith, let us strip off every weight that slows us down, especially the sin that so easily hinders our progress. And let us run with endurance the race that God has set before us. We do this by keeping our eyes on Jesus, on whom our faith depends from start to finish. He was willing to die a shameful death on the cross because of the joy he knew would be his afterward. Now he is seated in the place of highest honor beside God's throne in heaven. Think about all he endured when sinful people did such terrible things to him, so that you don't become weary and give up. After all, you have not yet given your lives in your struggle against sin. ❖ May the Lord bring you into an ever deeper understanding of the love of God and the endurance that comes from Christ. (Hebrews 12:1-4; 2 Thessalonians 3:5)

TAKEAWAY

Let us run with patience the particular race that God has set before us.

POWERTHOUGHT Despair is the vinegar from the wine of hope.—AUSTIN O'MALLEY, *Keystones of Thought*

Twenty-six

I WORRY:
LIFE SEEMS SO UNFAIR

☐ 176 _____

He maketh his sun to rise on the evil and on the good, and sendeth rain on the just and on the unjust. (Matthew 5:45, KJV)

TAKEAWAY
He sendeth rain on the just and on the unjust.

☐ 177 _____

Never envy the wicked! Soon they fade away like grass and disappear. ❖ There is not enough [wealth] in all the earth to buy eternal life for just one soul, to keep it out of hell. . . . Death is the shepherd of all mankind. And "in the morning" those who are evil will be the slaves of those who are good. . . . So do not be dismayed when evil men grow rich and build their lovely homes. (Psalms 37:1-2; 49:8-9, 14, 16, TLB)

TAKEAWAY
Do not be dismayed when evil men grow rich and build their lovely homes. For when they die, they carry nothing with them! (Psalm 49:16-17, TLB)

☐ 178 _____

How terrible it will be for you who lie awake at night, thinking up evil plans. You rise at dawn and hurry to carry out any of the wicked schemes you have power to accomplish. When you want a certain piece of land, you find a way to seize it. When you want someone's house, you take it by fraud and violence. No one's family or inheritance is safe with you around! ❖ For we know the one who said, "I will take vengeance. I will repay those who deserve it." He also said, "The Lord will judge his own people." (Micah 2:1-2; Hebrews 10:30)

TAKEAWAY
I will take vengeance. I will repay those who deserve it [says the Lord].

☐ 179 _____

We must all appear before the judgment seat of Christ. ❖ It is God that justifieth. (2 Corinthians 5:10; Romans 8:33, KJV)

TAKEAWAY
It is God that justifieth.

He was despised and rejected—a man of sorrows, acquainted with bitterest grief. We turned our backs on him and looked the other way when he went by. He was despised, and we did not care. Yet it was our weaknesses he carried; it was our sorrows that weighed him down. And we thought his troubles were a punishment from God for his own sins! But he was wounded and crushed for our sins. He was beaten that we might have peace. He was whipped, and we were healed! All of us have strayed away like sheep. We have left God's paths to follow our own. Yet the LORD laid on him the guilt and sins of us all. (Isaiah 53:3-6)

TAKEAWAY
He was wounded and bruised for *our* sins.

Dear friends, never avenge yourselves. Leave that to God. ❖ It is those who sow sin and trouble who harvest the same. They die beneath the hand of God. Though they are fierce as young lions, they shall all be broken and destroyed. (Romans 12:19; Job 4:8-10, TLB)

TAKEAWAY
Those who sow sin and trouble harvest the same.

Here is [a] story Jesus told: "The Kingdom of Heaven is like a farmer who planted good seed in his field. But that night as everyone slept, his enemy came and planted weeds among the wheat. When the crop began to grow and produce grain, the weeds also grew. The farmer's servants came and told him, 'Sir, the field where you planted that good seed is full of weeds!'" 'An enemy has done it!' the farmer exclaimed." 'Shall we pull out the weeds?' they asked. "He replied, 'No, you'll hurt the wheat if you do. Let both grow together until the harvest. Then I will tell the harvesters to sort out the weeds and burn them and to put the wheat in the barn.'". . . [Jesus'] disciples said, "Please explain the story of the weeds in the field." "All right," he said. "I, the Son of Man, am the farmer who plants the good seed. The field is the world, and the good seed represents the people of the Kingdom. The weeds are the people who belong to the evil one. The enemy who planted the weeds among the wheat is the Devil. The harvest is the end of the world, and the harvesters are the angels. "Just as the weeds are separated out and burned, so it will be at the end of the world. I, the Son of Man, will send my angels, and they will remove from my Kingdom everything that causes sin and all who do evil, and they will throw them into the furnace and burn them. There will be weeping and gnashing of teeth. Then the godly will shine like the sun in their Father's Kingdom. Anyone who is willing to hear should listen and understand!" (Matthew 13:24-30, 36-43)

TAKEAWAY
At the end of the world, the godly shall shine as the sun in their Father's Kingdom.

POWERTHOUGHT Let the world indulge its madness, for it cannot endure and passes like a shadow.—PETER CANISIUS (1521–1597)

The triumphing of the wicked is short, and the joy of the hypocrite but for a moment. —Job 20:5, KJV

Twenty-seven

I WORRY:
CAN GOD REALLY
CHANGE PEOPLE?

☐ 183 _____

O Lord, you are our Father. We are the clay and
you are the Potter. We are all formed by your hand.
❖ Here is another message to Jeremiah from the
Lord: Go down to the shop where clay pots and jars
are made, and I will talk to you there. I did as he
told me and found the potter working at his wheel.
But the jar that he was forming didn't turn out as he
wished, so he kneaded it into a lump and started
again. Then the Lord said: . . . Can't I do to you as
the potter has done to his clay? As the clay is in the
potter's hand, so you are in my hand. (Isaiah 64:8;
Jeremiah 18:1-6, TLB)

> TAKEAWAY
> We are the clay and the God of the universe is
> the Potter.

[Jesus said,] "Apart from me you can't do a thing."
❖ I will ask the Father, and he will give you another
to be your Advocate, who will be with you for
ever—the Spirit of truth. The world cannot receive
him, because the world neither sees nor knows him;
but you know him, because he dwells with you and
is in you. ❖ Christ in your hearts is your only hope
of glory. (John 15:5, TLB; John 14:15-17, NEB; Colossians 1:27, TLB)

TAKEAWAY

The literal translation of the word *Advocate* in
New Testament Greek is *Paraclete,* or "one who
comes alongside," or walks with us wherever we
go to provide support.

If I am doing what I don't want to do, I am not
really the one doing it; the sin within me is doing
it. . . . But there is another law at work within me
that is at war with my mind. This law wins the fight
and makes me a slave to the sin that is still within
me. Oh, what a miserable person I am! Who will
free me from this life that is dominated by sin?
Thank God! The answer is in Jesus Christ our Lord.
So you see how it is: In my mind I really want to
obey God's law, but because of my sinful nature I
am a slave to sin. So now there is no condemnation
for those who belong to Christ Jesus. For the power
of the life-giving Spirit has freed you through
Christ Jesus from the power of sin that leads to
death. The law of Moses could not save us, because

of our sinful nature. But God put into effect a different plan to save us. He sent his own Son in a human body like ours, except that ours are sinful. God destroyed sin's control over us by giving his Son as a sacrifice for our sins. He did this so that the requirement of the law would be fully accomplished for us who no longer follow our sinful nature but instead follow the Spirit. (Romans 7:20–8:4)

TAKEAWAY
So if the Son sets you free, you will indeed be free. (John 8:36)

☐ 186 _____

He who sat on the throne said, "Behold, I make all things new." (Revelation 21:5, NKJV)

TAKEAWAY
I make all things new.

☐ 187 _____

Jesus took Peter, James, and his brother John to the top of a high and lonely hill, and as they watched, his appearance changed so that his face shone like the sun and his clothing became dazzling white. . . . A bright cloud came over them, and a voice from the cloud said, "This is my beloved Son, and I am wonderfully pleased with him. Obey *him*." At this the disciples fell face downward to the ground, terribly frightened. Jesus came over and touched them. "Get up," he said, "don't be afraid." And when they looked, only Jesus was with them. (Matthew 17:1-2, 5-8, TLB)

Thank you, God, that you who were once trans-figured are powerful enough to transform me (and others), to fix what we have broken.

□ 188 _____

We are not ignorant of [Satan's] devices. ❖ Out of the heart proceed evil thoughts, murders, adulteries, fornications, thefts, false witness, blasphemies. These are the things which defile a man. ❖ Abhor what is evil. Cling to what is good. ❖ O LORD God . . . please give me success this day. (2 Corinthians 2:11; Matthew 15:19-20; Romans 12:9; Genesis 24:12, NKJV)

TAKEAWAY
What it lies in our power to do, it lies in our power not to do!—Aristotle (384–322 B.C.)

□ 189 _____

[Jesus said,] "I am the resurrection, and the life: he that believeth in me, though he were dead, yet shall he live." ❖ What this means is that those who become Christians become new persons. They are not the same anymore, for the old life is gone. A new life has begun! (John 11:25, KJV; 2 Corinthians 5:17)

TAKEAWAY
Jesus, by his death, resurrection, and ascension, is God's saving, life-changing gift to the world. He brings us back to God, rebirthing us and making us alive and whole again, even our innermost natures.

POWERTHOUGHT The LORD says, "I will rescue those who love me. I will protect those who trust in my name."
—Psalm 91:14

Twenty-eight

WHEN WORRY COMES, I WILL FOCUS ON GOD'S PAST HELP

☐ 190 _____

Every day I call to you, my God, but you do not answer. Every night you hear my voice, but I find no relief. Yet you are holy. The praises of Israel surround your throne. Our ancestors trusted in you, and you rescued them. . . . "Is this the one who relies on the LORD? Then let the LORD save him! If the LORD loves him so much, let the LORD rescue him!" Yet you brought me safely from my mother's womb and led me to trust you when I was a nursing infant. I was thrust upon you at my birth. You have been my God from the moment I was born. Do not stay so far from me, for trouble is near, and no one else can help me. . . . My life is poured out like water, and all my bones are out of joint. My heart is like wax, melting within me. . . . Snatch me from the lions' jaws, and from the horns of these wild oxen. Then I will declare the wonder of your name to my brothers and sisters. I will praise you among all your people. Praise the LORD, all you who fear him! Honor him, all you descendants of Jacob! Show him reverence, all you descendants of Israel! For he has not ignored the suffering of the needy. He has not turned and walked away. He has listened to their cries for help. . . . For the LORD is king! He rules all the nations. . . . His righteous acts will be told to those yet unborn. They will hear about everything he has done. (Psalm 22:2-4, 8-11, 14, 21-24, 28, 31) Recall a time when God helped out in a supernatural way. Record it here; then praise him for his help:

☐ 191 _____

I cried to him and he answered me! . . . The Angel of the Lord guards and rescues all who reverence him. Oh, put God to the test and see how kind he is! See for yourself the way his mercies shower down on all who trust in him. . . . For the eyes of the Lord are intently watching all who live good lives, and he gives attention when they cry to him. . . . Yes, the Lord hears the good man when he calls to him for help and saves him out of all his troubles. (Psalm 34:4, 7-8, 15-17, TLB) Recall a time when God helped out in a supernatural way. Record it here; then praise him for his help:

Bend down and listen to me; rescue me quickly. Be
for me a great rock of safety, a fortress where my
enemies cannot reach me. You are my rock and my
fortress. For the honor of your name, lead me out of
this peril. Pull me from the trap my enemies set for
me, for I find protection in you alone. I entrust my
spirit into your hand. Rescue me, LORD, for you are
a faithful God. (Psalm 31:2-5) Recall a time when
God helped out in a supernatural way. Record it
here; then praise him for his help:

The LORD lives! Praise be to my Rock! Exalted be
God my savior! ❖ O God, we have heard of the glorious miracles you did in the days of long ago. Our
forefathers have told us how you drove the heathen
nations from this land and gave it all to us. . . . They
did not conquer by their own strength and skill, but
by your mighty power and because you smiled
upon them and favored them. You are my King and
my God. . . . I do not trust my weapons. They could
never save me. Only you can give the victory over
those who hate us. My constant boast is God. I can
never thank you enough! (Psalm 18:46, NIV; Psalm
44:1-8, TLB) Recall a time when God helped out in a
supernatural way. Record it here; then praise him
for his help:

_____

In sudden fear I had cried out, "I have been cut off
from the LORD!" But you heard my cry for mercy
and answered my call for help. Love the LORD, all
you faithful ones! For the LORD protects those who
are loyal to him, but he harshly punishes all who are
arrogant. So be strong and take courage, all you
who put your hope in the LORD! (Psalm 31:22-24)
Recall a time when God helped out in a supernatural way. Record it here; then praise him for his help:

_____

Come and listen, all you who fear God, and I will
tell you what he did for me. For I cried out to him
for help, praising him as I spoke. If I had not con-
fessed the sin in my heart, my Lord would not have
listened. But God did listen! He paid attention to
my prayer. Praise God, who did not ignore my
prayer and did not withdraw his unfailing love from
me. (Psalm 66:16-20) Recall a time when God
helped out in a supernatural way. Record it here;
then praise him for his help:

_____

Death bound me with chains, and the floods of
ungodliness mounted a massive attack against me.
Trapped and helpless, I struggled against the ropes
that drew me on to death. In my distress I screamed
to the Lord for his help. And he heard me from

heaven; my cry reached his ears. . . . Suddenly the brilliance of his presence broke through the clouds with lightning and a mighty storm of hail. The Lord thundered in the heavens; the God above all gods has spoken—oh, the hailstones; oh, the fire! He flashed his fearful arrows of lightning and routed all my enemies. See how they run! . . . He reached down from heaven and took me and drew me out of my great trials. He rescued me from deep waters. (Psalm 18:4-6, 12-16, TLB) Recall a time when God helped out in a supernatural way. Record it here; then praise him for his help:

POWERTHOUGHT I am the LORD, I change not.
—Malachi 3:6, KJV

Twenty-nine

WHEN WORRY COMES, I'LL REMEMBER WHOSE I AM

☐ 197 _____

Everyone who believes that Jesus is the Christ is a child of God. And everyone who loves the Father loves his children, too. (1 John 5:1)

TAKEAWAY
I bear his name. I am a child of God.

☐ 198 _____

When the right time came, God sent his Son . . . to buy freedom for us who were slaves to the law, so that he could adopt us as his very own children. And because you Gentiles have become his children, God has sent the Spirit of his Son into your hearts, and now you can call God your dear Father. ❖ He has identified us as his own by placing the

Holy Spirit in our hearts as the first installment of everything he will give us. (Galatians 4:4-6; 2 Corinthians 1:22)

TAKEAWAY
We can rightly speak of God as Father.

☐ 199 _____

Because of what Christ has done, we have become gifts to God that he delights in, for as part of God's sovereign plan we were chosen from the beginning to be his. . . . I want you to realize that God has been made rich because we who are Christ's have been given to him! (Ephesians 1:11, 18, TLB)

TAKEAWAY
I am a gift to God that he delights in.

☐ 200 _____

All honor to the God and Father of our Lord Jesus Christ, for it is by his boundless mercy that God has given us the privilege of being born again. Now we live with a wonderful expectation because Jesus Christ rose again from the dead. ❖ So now Jesus and the ones he makes holy have the same Father. That is why Jesus is not ashamed to call them his brothers and sisters. ❖ His purpose in all of this was that the nations should seek after God and perhaps feel their way toward him and find him—though he is not far from any one of us. For in him we live and move and exist. As one of your own poets says, "We are his offspring." (1 Peter 1:3; Hebrews 2:11; Acts 17:27-28)

☐ 201 _____

[Jesus said,] "The Father himself loves you dearly because you love me and believe that I came from the Father." ❖ All who are led by the Spirit of God are sons of God. And so we should not be like cringing, fearful slaves, but we should behave like God's very own children, adopted into the bosom of his family, and calling to him, "Father, Father." (John 16:27; Romans 8:14-15, TLB)

> T A K E A W A Y
> The Lord said to me, "I knew you before you were formed within your mother's womb." (Jeremiah 1:4-5, TLB)

☐ 202 _____

Our lives are a fragrance presented by Christ to God. But this fragrance is perceived differently by those being saved and by those perishing. ❖ So now you Gentiles are no longer strangers and foreigners. You are citizens along with all of God's holy people. You are members of God's family. We are his house, built on the foundation of the apostles and the prophets. And the cornerstone is Christ Jesus himself. (2 Corinthians 2:15; Ephesians 2:19-20)

> T A K E A W A Y
> As far as God is concerned, there is a sweet, wholesome fragrance in our lives.

I created you and have cared for you since before you were born. ❖ For the LORD your God has arrived to live among you. He is a mighty savior. He will rejoice over you with great gladness. With his love, he will calm all your fears. He will exult over you by singing a happy song. (Isaiah 46:3; Zephaniah 3:17)

T A K E A W A Y
The Lord loves me. He exults over me in happy song! Me! Incredible!

POWERTHOUGHT We are God's household, if we keep up our courage and remain confident in our hope in Christ.—Hebrews 3:6

Thirty

WHEN WORRY COMES, I HAVE THE ULTIMATE FRIEND

☐ 204 _____

[Jesus said,] "The greatest love is shown when people lay down their lives for their friends. You are my friends if you obey me." (John 15:13-14)

TAKEAWAY
I can trust a friend who would die for me.

☐ 205 _____

By [Christ] God reconciled everything to himself. He made peace with everything in heaven and on earth by means of his blood on the cross. This includes you who were once so far away from God. You were his enemies, separated from him by your evil thoughts and actions, yet now he has brought you back as his friends. He has done this through his death on the cross in his own human body. As a result, he has brought you into the very presence of God, and you are holy and blameless as you stand before him without a single fault. But you must continue to believe this truth and stand in it firmly. Don't drift away from the assurance you received when you heard the Good News. The Good News has been preached all over the world, and I, Paul, have been appointed by God to proclaim it. (Colossians 1:20-23)

TAKEAWAY

He calls his own sheep by name and leads them out. (John 10:3)

□ 206 _____

Friendship with the LORD is reserved for those who fear him. With them he shares the secrets of his covenant. ❖ [Jesus said,] "I am the good shepherd; I know my own sheep, and they know me. . . . My sheep recognize my voice; I know them, and they follow me. I give them eternal life, and they will never perish. No one will snatch them away from me, for my Father has given them to me, and he is more powerful than anyone else. So no one can take them from me." (Psalm 25:14; John 10:14, 27-29)

TAKEAWAY

I have written your name on my hand. (Isaiah 49:16)

□ 207 _____

A true friend is always loyal, and a brother is born to help in time of need. ❖ There are "friends" who destroy each other, but a real friend sticks closer than a brother. ❖ [Jesus promised,] "Lo, I am with you alway, even unto the end of the world." ❖ If I ascend into heaven, You are there; if I make my bed in hell, behold, You are there. ❖ I am persuaded that neither death nor life, nor angels nor principalities nor powers, nor things present nor things to come, nor height nor depth, nor any other created thing, shall be able to separate us from the love of God which is in Christ Jesus our Lord. (Proverbs 17:17, TLB; Proverbs 18:24; Matthew 28:20, KJV; Psalm 139:8; Romans 8:38-39, NKJV)

TAKEAWAY
My friend God is a very *present* help in trouble. (Paraphrase of Psalm 46:1)

☐ 208 _____

The LORD your God which goeth before you, he shall fight for you. ❖ Who shall separate us from the love of Christ? ❖ I will be with you, and I will protect you wherever you go. ❖ Be strong and courageous! . . . Do not be afraid or discouraged, for the LORD is the one who goes before you. . . . He will neither fail you nor forsake you. ❖ Even if my father and mother abandon me, the LORD will hold me close. ❖ Look! The virgin will conceive a child! She will give birth to a son, and he will be called Immanuel (meaning, God is with us). ❖ No, I will not abandon you as orphans—I will come to you. ❖ The God of love and peace will be with you. (Deuteronomy 1:30; Romans 8:35, KJV; Genesis 28:15; Deuteronomy

31:7-8; Psalm 27:10; Matthew 1:23; John 14:18; 2 Corinthians 13:11)

TAKEAWAY
My friend God is with me—*now!*

☐ 209 _____

I am the Vine; you are the branches. . . . Live within my love. . . . You are my friends, proved by the fact that I have told you everything the Father told me. You didn't choose me! I chose you! (John 15:5, 9, 15-16, TLB)

TAKEAWAY
My friend God chose me.

☐ 210 _____

Fear not, for I have redeemed you; I have summoned you by name; you are mine. ❖ He knoweth them that trust in him. ❖ I know thee by name. ❖ Behold, I am for you, and I will turn unto you. ❖ I know the thoughts that I think toward you, saith the LORD, thoughts of peace, and not of evil, to give you an expected end. ❖ God is my helper. The Lord is the one who keeps me alive! ❖ The curse of the LORD is on the house of the wicked, but his blessing is on the home of the upright. (Isaiah 43:1, NIV; Nahum 1:7; Exodus 33:17; Ezekiel 36:9; Jeremiah 29:11, KJV; Psalm 54:4; Proverbs 3:33)

TAKEAWAY
My ultimate Friend knows me by name.

POWERTHOUGHT Christ has entered into heaven itself to appear now before God as our Friend.—Hebrews 9:24, TLB

Picture yourself as God's friend. Can you see him looking at you with love? Are you remembering that he wants the best for you? Are you remembering that he saw you and loved you long ago in your mother's womb?

Thirty-one

WHEN WORRY COMES, I WILL LIVE ONE DAY AT A TIME

☐ 211 _____

God saw every thing that he had made, and, behold, it was very good. ❖ This is the day which the Lord hath made; we will rejoice and be glad in it. (Genesis 1:31; Psalm 118:24, KJV)

TAKEAWAY
Every morning, lean thine arms awhile
Upon the windowsill of Heaven,
And gaze upon the Lord . . .
Then, with that vision in thy heart,
Turn strong to meet the day.
                                    —Unknown Author

Thou knowest not what a day may bring forth. ❖
This I know; for God is for me. ❖ So take courage!
For I believe God. It will be just as he said. (Prov-
erbs 27:1; Psalm 56:9, KJV; Acts 27:25)

TAKEAWAY
**I will extol thee, my God. . . . Every day will I
bless thee. (Psalm 145:1-2, KJV)**

The day is mine to mar or make,
God keep me strong and true;
Let me no erring by-path take,
No doubtful action do.

Grant me when the setting sun
This fleeting day shall end,
I may rejoice o'er something done,
Be richer by a friend.

Let all I meet along the way
Speak well of me to-night.
I would not have the humblest say
I'd hurt him by a slight.

Let there be something true and fine
When night slips down to tell
That I have lived this day of mine
Not selfishly, but well.

—ANONYMOUS

TAKEAWAY
Make this minute a good one.

[God] understands how weak we are; he knows we are only dust. Our days on earth are like grass; like wildflowers, we bloom and die. The wind blows, and we are gone—as though we had never been here. But the love of the LORD remains forever with those who fear him. (Psalm 103:14-17)

TAKEAWAY
Even if I live to be seventy, my life will contain only about twenty-five thousand days. Each comes one at a time. Each is so short, and there are so few. Lord, help me love each day, to embrace it as a wonderful thing, as a gift, and not to waste it in misery or futility.

How to Have a Good Day:

The peace of God, which surpasses all understanding, will guard your hearts and minds through Christ Jesus. . . . Whatever things are true, whatever things are noble, whatever things are just, whatever things are pure, whatever things are lovely, whatever things are of good report, if there is any virtue and if there is anything praiseworthy—meditate on these things. (Philippians 4:7-8, NKJV)

TAKEAWAY
Fill your mind with thoughts that are true, noble, just, pure, and lovely.

To miss the joy is to miss all.—ROBERT LOUIS
STEVENSON

God works in moments.—FRENCH PROVERB

TAKEAWAY
You say, "This World to you seems drain'd of its
sweets!" I don't know what you call sweet. Honey
and the honeycomb, roses and violets, are yet in
the earth. The sun and moon yet reign in
Heaven, and the lesser lights keep up their pretty
twinklings. Meats and drinks, sweet sights and
sweet smells, a country walk, spring and autumn,
follies and repentance, quarrels and reconcile-
ments have all a sweetness by turns. Good humour
and good nature, friends at home that love you,
and friends abroad that miss you—you possess all
these things, and more innumerable, and these
are all sweet things. You may extract honey from
everything.—Charles Lamb (1775–1834)

He hath put a new song in my mouth, even praise
unto our God. ❖ I will sing of thy power; yea, I will
sing aloud of thy mercy in the morning. ❖ Surely
goodness and mercy shall follow me all the days of
my life. (Psalms 40:3, 59:16, 23:6, KJV)

TAKEAWAY
The Lord himself is my inheritance, my prize. He
is my food and drink, my highest joy! He guards
all that is mine. He sees that I am given pleasant

brooks and meadows as my share! What a wonderful inheritance! I will bless the Lord.
(Psalm 16:5-7, TLB)

POWERTHOUGHT A single constant affirmation that the everlasting arms of God are holding you up, repeated hour by hour until you become convinced that God is now your guide and stay, will often bring you out of worries and fears, but how many Christians will really let go their fears and let God handle them? The only complete cure for your bad nerves, as you call them, is to relax in the hands of God and know that He is now looking after your troubles, that He is now guiding you into the quiet waters of inner peace.

—NORMAN VINCENT PEALE,
A Treasury of Courage and Confidence

Thirty-two

WHEN WORRY COMES, I WILL MEDITATE ON GOD'S INCREDIBLE POWER TO HELP

☐ 218 _____

He sits enthroned above the circle of the earth. . . .
"To whom will you compare me? Or who is my
equal?" says the Holy One. Lift your eyes and look to
the heavens: Who created all these? He who brings
out the starry host one by one, and calls them each
by name. Because of his great power and mighty
strength, not one of them is missing. . . . Do you not
know? Have you not heard? The LORD is the everlasting God, the Creator of the ends of the earth. He
will not grow tired or weary. (Isaiah 40:22-28, NIV)

TAKEAWAY
**Lift your eyes and look to the heavens: Who cre-
ated all these?**

The Sovereign LORD is coming in all his glorious power. He will rule with awesome strength. See, he brings his reward with him as he comes. . . . Who else has held the oceans in his hand? Who has measured off the heavens with his fingers? Who else knows the weight of the earth or has weighed out the mountains and the hills? Who is able to advise the Spirit of the LORD? Who knows enough to be his teacher or counselor? (Isaiah 40:10-13)

TAKEAWAY

Who else [but God] has held the oceans in his hand? Who has measured off the heavens with his fingers?

☐ 220

Lord, through all the generations you have been our home! Before the mountains were created, before the earth was formed, you are God without beginning or end. You speak, and man turns back to dust. A thousand years are but as yesterday to you! They are like a single hour! (Psalm 90:1-4, TLB)

TAKEAWAY

Before the mountains were created, before the earth was formed, you are God, without beginning or end. You speak and man turns back to dust.

☐ 221

Oh, that you would burst from the heavens and come down! How the mountains would quake in your presence! As fire causes wood to burn and water to boil, your coming would make the nations tremble. Then your enemies would learn the reason for your fame! When you came down long ago, you did awesome things beyond our highest expectations. And oh, how the mountains quaked! For since the world began, no ear has heard, and no eye has seen a God like you, who works for those who wait for him! (Isaiah 64:1-4)

TAKEAWAY

Oh, that you would burst forth from the skies and come down! The consuming fire of your glory would burn down the forests and boil the oceans dry.

☐ 222 _____

Who in the heaven can be compared unto the LORD? . . . O LORD God of hosts, who is a strong LORD like unto thee? . . . Thou rulest the raging of the sea: when the waves thereof arise, thou stillest them. . . . The heavens are thine, the earth also is thine: as for the world and the fulness thereof, thou has founded them. The north and the south thou hast created them. . . . Thou hast a mighty arm: strong is thy hand, and high is thy right hand. . . . Blessed is the people that . . . walk, O LORD, in the light of thy countenance. . . . For thou art the glory of their strength: and in thy favour our horn shall be exalted. (Psalm 89:6-17, KJV)

TAKEAWAY

O Lord God of hosts, thou rulest the raging sea. When the waves arise, thou stillest them.

God stands beside you to protect you. ❖ Because
the Lord God helps me, I will not be dismayed;
therefore, I have set my face like flint to do his will,
and I know that I will triumph. He who gives me
justice is near. Who will dare to fight against me
now? Where are my enemies? Let them appear! See,
the Lord God is for me! Who shall declare me
guilty? All my enemies shall be destroyed like old
clothes eaten up by moths! (Psalm 110:5; Isaiah
50:7-9, TLB)

> *TAKEAWAY*
> **God stands beside me to protect me. See the
> Lord God is *for* me!**

O LORD, what a variety of things you have made! In
wisdom you have made them all. The earth is full of
your creatures. Here is the ocean, vast and wide,
teeming with life of every kind, both great and
small. See the ships sailing along, and Leviathan,
which you made to play in the sea. Every one of
these depends on you to give them their food as
they need it. When you supply it, they gather it.
You open your hand to feed them, and they are satisfied. But if you turn away from them, they panic.
When you take away their breath, they die and turn
again to dust. When you send your Spirit, new life
is born to replenish all the living of the earth. May
the glory of the LORD last forever! The LORD
rejoices in all he has made! (Psalm 104:24-31)

The earth is full of your riches—the mighty ocean teeming with life of every kind.

POWERTHOUGHT There is something almost ludicrous in sitting down at a desk and writing the word "God" and then being presumptuous enough to add anything.
—LESLIE WEATHERHEAD, *The Christian Agnostic*

Thirty-three

STANDING UP TO ANXIETY

☐ 225 _____

Give all your worries and cares to God, for he cares about what happens to you. (1 Peter 5:7)

TAKEAWAY
He is watching over everything that concerns you.

☐ 226 _____

Now glory be to God! By his mighty power at work within us, he is able to accomplish infinitely more than we would ever dare to ask or hope. May he be given glory in the church and in Christ Jesus forever and ever through endless ages. (Ephesians 3:20-21)

He is able to accomplish infinitely more than we would ever dare to ask or hope.

☐ 227 _____

Can all your worries add a single moment to your life? Of course not! ❖ How can we understand the road we travel? It is the LORD who directs our steps. (Luke 12:25; Proverbs 20:24)

Worrying will not add a single moment to your life.

☐ 228 _____

Christ is not weak in his dealings with you but is a mighty power within you. His weak, human body died on the cross, but now he lives by the mighty power of God. We, too, are weak in our bodies, as he was, but now we live and are strong, as he is, and have all of God's power to use. (2 Corinthians 13:3-4, TLB)

We have all of God's power to use in times of trouble.

☐ 229 _____

Always be full of joy in the Lord. I say it again—rejoice! . . . Don't worry about anything; instead, pray about everything. Tell God what you need, and thank him for all he has done. If you do this, you will experience God's peace, which is far more wonderful than the human mind can understand. His peace will guard your hearts and minds as you live in Christ Jesus. (Philippians 4:4-7)

TAKEAWAY

Pray about everything. Tell God your needs. If you do this, you will experience God's peace.

☐ 230 _____

All who are led by the Spirit of God are sons of God. And so we should not be like cringing, fearful slaves, but we should behave like God's very own children, adopted into the bosom of his family, and calling to him, "Father, Father." ❖ "Don't be afraid. . . . For I am with you," says the Lord. (Romans 8:14-15; Jeremiah 1:17-19, TLB)

TAKEAWAY

We should not be like cringing, fearful slaves. "I am with you," says the Lord.

☐ 231 _____

Open the gates to all who are righteous; allow the faithful to enter. You will keep in perfect peace all who trust in you, whose thoughts are fixed on you! Trust in the LORD always, for the LORD GOD is the eternal Rock. (Isaiah 26:2-4)

TAKEAWAY

Turn your thoughts often to the Lord Jehovah.

POWERTHOUGHT Anxiety in human life is what squeaking and grinding are in machines that is not oiled. In life, trust is the oil.—HENRY WARD BEECHER, *Proverbs from Plymouth Pulpit*

Thirty-four

STANDING UP TO FEAR

☐ 232 _____

I look up to the mountains—does my help come from there? My help comes from the LORD, who made the heavens and the earth! He will not let you stumble and fall; the one who watches over you will not sleep. Indeed, he who watches over Israel never tires and never sleeps. The LORD himself watches over you! The LORD stands beside you as your protective shade. The sun will not hurt you by day, nor the moon at night. The LORD keeps you from all evil and preserves your life. The LORD keeps watch over you as you come and go, both now and forever. (Psalm 121)

TAKEAWAY
He keeps his eye upon you as you come and go.

I've commanded you to be strong and brave. Don't ever be afraid or discouraged! I am the LORD your God, and I will be there to help you wherever you go. (Joshua 1:9, CEV)

TAKEAWAY
I am the Lord your God, and I will be there to help you wherever you go.

The LORD is my light and my salvation—so why should I be afraid? The LORD protects me from danger—so why should I tremble? When evil people come to destroy me, when my enemies and foes attack me, they will stumble and fall. Though a mighty army surrounds me, my heart will know no fear. Even if they attack me, I remain confident. . . . Listen to my pleading, O LORD. Be merciful and answer me! (Psalm 27:1-3, 7)

TAKEAWAY
Though a mighty army marches against me, my heart shall know no fear!

God is my helper. He is a friend of mine! (Psalm 54:4, TLB)

TAKEAWAY
God is my helper. He is a friend of mine!

This I declare of the LORD: He alone is my refuge, my place of safety; he is my God, and I am trusting him. For he will rescue you from every trap and protect you from the fatal plague. . . . Do not be afraid of the terrors of the night, nor fear the dangers of the day, nor dread the plague that stalks in darkness, nor the disaster that strikes at midday. Though a thousand fall at your side, though ten thousand are dying around you, these evils will not touch you. . . . If you make the LORD your refuge, if you make the Most High your shelter, no evil will conquer you; no plague will come near your dwelling. (Psalm 91:2-10)

TAKEAWAY

He alone is my refuge, my place of safety; he is my God, and I am trusting him.

Tell the LORD how thankful you are, because he is kind and always merciful. . . . When I was really hurting, I prayed to the LORD. He answered my prayer, and took my worries away. The LORD is on my side, and I am not afraid of what others can do to me. With the LORD on my side, I will defeat all of my hateful enemies. It is better to trust the LORD for protection than to trust anyone else, including strong leaders. . . . My power and my strength come from the LORD, and he has saved me. From the tents of God's people come shouts of victory: "The LORD is powerful! With his mighty arm the LORD wins victories! The LORD is powerful!" And so my life is safe. (Psalm 118:1, 5-9, 14-17, CEV)

**The Lord is on my side, and I am not afraid of
what others can do to me. The Lord is powerful!
The Lord wins victories!**

☐ 238 _____

Fear not, for I have redeemed you; I have called you
by your name. You are Mine. When you pass
through the waters, I will be with you; and through
the rivers, they shall not overflow you. . . . Fear not,
for I am with you. . . . Thus says the LORD, who
makes a way in the sea and a path through the
mighty waters. (Isaiah 43:1-2, 5, 16, NKJV)

T A K E A W A Y
**Fear not, for I am with you. Thus says the Lord
who makes a path through mighty waters.**

POWERTHOUGHT

Some of your hurts you have cured,
 And the sharpest you still have survived;
But what torments of grief you endured
 From evils which never arrived.
—RALPH WALDO EMERSON, *Borrowings*

Thirty-five

STANDING UP TO THE STRAIN OF SICKNESS

☐ 239 _____

Be merciful to me, LORD, for I am faint; O LORD, heal me, for my bones are in agony. My soul is in anguish. How long, O LORD, how long? Turn, O LORD, and deliver me; save me because of your unfailing love. . . . I am worn out from groaning; all night long I flood my bed with weeping and drench my couch with tears. My eyes grow weak with sorrow. . . . The LORD has heard my cry for mercy; the LORD accepts my prayer. . . . O LORD my God, I take refuge in you. (Psalms 6:2–7:1, NIV)

TAKEAWAY
O Lord, I am faint. Heal me. I take refuge in you.

☐ 240 _____

What is impossible from a human perspective is possible with God. (Luke 18:27)

☐ 241 _____

As they approached Jericho, a blind beggar was sitting beside the road. When he heard the noise of a crowd going past, he asked what was happening. They told him that Jesus of Nazareth was going by. So he began shouting, "Jesus, Son of David, have mercy on me!" The crowds ahead of Jesus tried to hush the man, but he only shouted louder, "Son of David, have mercy on me!" When Jesus heard him, he stopped and ordered that the man be brought to him. Then Jesus asked the man, "What do you want me to do for you? "Lord," he pleaded, "I want to see!" And Jesus said, "All right, you can see! Your faith has healed you." Instantly the man could see, and he followed Jesus, praising God. And all who saw it praised God, too. (Luke 18:35-43)

TAKEAWAY
Jesus Christ is the same yesterday and today, yes and forever. (Hebrews 13:8, NASB)

☐ 242 _____

I want to remind you that your strength must come from the Lord's mighty power within you. ❖ I want you to trust me in your times of trouble, so I can rescue you and you can give me glory. (Ephesians 6:10; Psalm 50:15, TLB)

Trust me in your times of trouble, so I can rescue you and you can give me glory.

☐ 243 _____

I am scorned by all my enemies and despised by my neighbors—even my friends are afraid to come near me. When they see me on the street, they turn the other way. I have been ignored as if I were dead, as if I were a broken pot. ❖ On the very day I call to you for help, my enemies will retreat. This I know: God is on my side. O God, I praise your word. Yes, LORD, I praise your word. (Psalms 31:11-12; 56:9-10)

TAKEAWAY
O Lord, have mercy upon me in my anguish. This one thing I know: God is for me!

☐ 244 _____

A thorn in the flesh was given to me, a messenger of Satan to buffet me, lest I be exalted above measure. Concerning this thing I pleaded with the Lord three times that it might depart from me. And He said to me, "My grace is sufficient for you, for My strength is made perfect in weakness." Therefore most gladly I will rather boast in my infirmities, that the power of Christ may rest upon me. . . . For when I am weak, then I am strong. (2 Corinthians 12:7-10, NKJV)

TAKEAWAY
My grace is sufficient for you.—The Lord

A cheerful heart is good medicine, but a broken spirit saps a person's strength. ❖ Don't be impressed with your own wisdom. Instead, fear the LORD and turn your back on evil. Then you will gain renewed health and vitality. (Proverbs 17:22; 3:7-8)

TAKEAWAY
Trust and reverence the Lord, and turn your back on evil; when you do that, then you will be given renewed health and vitality.

POWERTHOUGHT

God moves in a mysterious way
His wonders to perform;
He plants his footsteps in the sea
And rides upon the storm.

You fearful saints, fresh courage take:
The clouds you so much dread
Are big with mercy, and shall break
In blessings on your head.

Judge not the Lord by feeble sense,
But trust him for his grace;
Behind a frowning providence
He hides a smiling face.

—WILLIAM COWPER (1731–1800)

Thirty-six

STANDING UP TO STRESS

☐ 246 _____

I wait quietly before God, for my salvation comes
from him. He alone is my rock and my salvation,
my fortress where I will never be shaken. (Psalm
62:1-2)

> **TAKEAWAY**
> He alone is my rock and my salvation, my fortress
> where I will never be shaken.

☐ 247 _____

O God, listen to my cry! Hear my prayer! From the
ends of the earth, I will cry to you for help, for my
heart is overwhelmed. Lead me to the towering
rock of safety, for you are my safe refuge, a fortress
where my enemies cannot reach me. . . . Then I will

always sing praises to your name as I fulfill my vows day after day. (Psalm 61:1-3, 8)

> TAKEAWAY
> **Wherever I am, though far away at the ends of the earth, you are my refuge.**

□ 248 _____

O LORD, you are my light; yes, LORD, you light up my darkness. In your strength I can crush an army; with my God I can scale any wall. As for God, his way is perfect. All the LORD's promises prove true. He is a shield for all who look to him for protection. For who is God except the LORD? Who but our God is a solid rock? (2 Samuel 22:29-32)

> TAKEAWAY
> **Lord, you are my light! You make my darkness bright!**

□ 249 _____

God is my strong fortress; he has made my way safe. He makes me as surefooted as a deer, leading me safely along the mountain heights. . . . You have given me the shield of your salvation; your help has made me great. You have made a wide path for my feet to keep them from slipping. (2 Samuel 22:33-37)

> TAKEAWAY
> **God, you have made wide steps for my feet, to keep them from slipping.**

He telleth the number of the stars; he calleth them
all by their names. Great is our Lord, and of great
power. ❖ They took him . . . in the ship. . . . And
there arose a great storm of wind, and the waves
beat into the ship, so that it was now full. And he
was in the hinder part of the ship, asleep on a pillow: and they awake[ned] him, and say unto him,
Master, carest thou not that we perish? And he
arose, and rebuked the wind, and said unto the
sea, Peace, be still. And the wind ceased, and there
was a great calm. And he said unto them, Why are
ye so fearful? how is it that ye have no faith? And
they feared exceedingly, and said one to another,
What manner of man is this that even the wind
and the sea obey him? (Psalm 147:4-5; Mark 4:36-
41, KJV)

TAKEAWAY

**Great is our Lord, and of great power. Why are
you so fearful? Even the wind and the sea obey
him!**

When I am afraid, I put my trust in you. O God, I
praise your word. I trust in God, so why should I be
afraid? What can mere mortals do to me? . . . I trust
in God, so why should I be afraid? What can mere
mortals do to me? I will fulfill my vows to you,
O God, and offer a sacrifice of thanks for your help.
(Psalm 56:3-4, 11-12)

When I am afraid, I will trust in the promises of God.

☐ 252 _____

My days disappear like smoke, and my bones burn like red-hot coals. My heart is sick, withered like grass, and I have lost my appetite. . . . I lie awake, lonely as a solitary bird on the roof. ❖ Always be full of joy in the Lord. I say it again—rejoice! . . . Don't worry about anything; instead, pray about everything. Tell God what you need, and thank him for all he has done. (Psalm 102:3-4, 7; Philippians 4:4, 6)

TAKEAWAY
Pray about everything.

POWERTHOUGHT Our Lord did not try to alter circumstances. He submitted to them. They shaped his life and eventually brought him to Calvary. I believe we miss opportunities and lovely secrets our Lord is waiting to teach us by not taking what comes.—MOTHER MARIABEL, CSMV

Thirty-seven

STANDING UP TO DISCOURAGEMENT

☐ 253 _____

Griping brings discouragement. ❖ I will pray morning, noon, and night, pleading aloud with God; and he will hear and answer. Though the tide of battle runs strongly against me, for so many are fighting me, yet he will rescue me. . . . Give your burdens to the Lord. He will carry them. He will not permit the godly to slip or fall. (Proverbs 15:4; Psalm 55:17-18, 22, TLB)

TAKEAWAY
Troubles will come, which seem as if they never would pass away. The night and storm look as if they would last forever; but the calm and the morning cannot be stayed; the storm in its very nature is transient. The effort of nature, as that of the human heart, ever is to return to its repose, for God is Peace.—George Macdonald

Why am I discouraged? Why so sad? I will put my hope in God! I will praise him again—my Savior and my God! (Psalm 43:5)

TAKEAWAY

He will make me smile again, for he is my God!

I will praise the LORD at all times. I will constantly speak his praises. I will boast only in the LORD; let all who are discouraged take heart. Come, let us tell of the LORD's greatness; let us exalt his name together. (Psalm 34:1-3)

TAKEAWAY

I will praise the Lord no matter what happens.

And now, just as you accepted Christ Jesus as your Lord, you must continue to live in obedience to him. Let your roots grow down into him and draw up nourishment from him, so you will grow in faith, strong and vigorous in the truth you were taught. Let your lives overflow with thanksgiving for all he has done. ❖ So be truly glad! There is wonderful joy ahead, even though it is necessary for you to endure many trials for a while. (Colossians 2:6-7; 1 Peter 1:6)

Let your roots grow down into him and draw up nourishment from him. There is wonderful joy ahead.

☐ 257 _____

I sank beneath the waves, and death was very near. The waters closed in around me, and seaweed wrapped itself around my head. I sank down to the very roots of the mountains. I was locked out of life and imprisoned in the land of the dead. But you, O LORD my God, have snatched me from the yawning jaws of death! When I had lost all hope, I turned my thoughts once more to the LORD. And my earnest prayer went out to you in your holy Temple. Those who worship false gods turn their backs on all God's mercies. (Jonah 2:5-8)

T A K E A W A Y
When I lose all hope, I will turn my thoughts to the Lord.

☐ 258 _____

God has said, "I will never, *never* fail you nor forsake you." That is why we can say without any doubt or fear, "The Lord is my Helper, and I am not afraid of anything that mere man can do to me." (Hebrews 13:5-6, TLB)

T A K E A W A Y
God has said, "I will never, *never* fail you nor forsake you."

From discouragement to praise: Do not hide yourself from me. Do not reject your servant in anger.
You have always been my helper. Don't leave me
now; don't abandon me, O God of my salvation! ❖
O Lord, what miracles you do! And how deep are
your thoughts! . . . The Lord continues forever,
exalted in the heavens. . . . You have made me as
strong as a wild bull. How refreshed I am by your
blessings! I have heard the doom of my enemies an-
nounced and seen them destroyed. But the godly
shall flourish like palm trees and grow tall as the
cedars of Lebanon. (Psalms 27:9; 92:5-12, TLB)

TAKEAWAY
**You have been my help in all my trials before.
How refreshed I am by your blessings!**

POWERTHOUGHT Birds sing after a storm. Why
shouldn't people feel as free to delight in whatever remains
to them?—ROSE KENNEDY, *Times to Remember*

Thirty-eight

STANDING UP TO "THE BLUES"

☐ 260 _____

Take courage, my soul! . . . Why be discouraged and sad? Hope in God! I shall yet praise him again. Yes, I shall again praise him for his help. Yet I am standing here depressed and gloomy, but I will meditate upon your kindness. . . . All your waves and billows have gone over me, and floods of sorrow pour upon me like a thundering cataract. Yet day by day the Lord also pours out his steadfast love upon me, and through the night I sing his songs and pray to God who gives me life. . . . O my soul, don't be discouraged. Don't be upset. Expect God to act! For I know that I shall again have plenty of reason to praise him for all that he will do. He is my help! He is my God! (Psalm 42:4-8, 11, TLB)

TAKEAWAY
"Take courage my soul! . . . Why be discouraged and sad? Hope in God!"

I Will Praise God Anyway: This is the day the LORD has made; let us rejoice and be glad in it. ❖ Shout for joy to the LORD, all the earth, burst into jubilant song with music; make music to the LORD with the harp, with the harp and the sound of singing, with trumpets and the blast of the ram's horn—shout for joy before the LORD, the King. Let the sea resound, and everything in it, the world, and all who live in it. Let the rivers clap their hands, let the mountains sing together for joy; let them sing before the LORD. (Psalms 118:24; 98:4-9, NIV)

TAKEAWAY
Two men looked out through prison bars.
The one saw mud; the other stars.—Author
Unknown

My health may fail, and my spirit may grow weak, but God remains the strength of my heart; he is mine forever. ❖ But I will keep on hoping for you to help me; I will praise you more and more. I will tell everyone about your righteousness. All day long I will proclaim your saving power, for I am over-whelmed by how much you have done for me. ❖ When doubts filled my mind, your comfort gave me renewed hope and cheer. . . . But the LORD is my fortress; my God is a mighty rock where I can hide. ❖ Don't be dejected and sad, for the joy of the LORD is your strength! (Psalms 73:26; 71:14-15; 94:19, 22; Nehemiah 8:10)

☐ 263 _____

I Will Pray My Way through the Gloom: Are any among you suffering? They should keep on praying about it. . . . Are any among you sick? They should call for the elders of the church and have them pray over them, anointing them with oil in the name of the Lord. . . . The earnest prayer of a righteous person has great power and wonderful results. Elijah was as human as we are, and yet when he prayed earnestly that no rain would fall, none fell for the next three and a half years! Then he prayed for rain, and down it poured. The grass turned green, and the crops began to grow again. ❖ I know that you [the Lord] can do anything, and no one can stop you. ❖ We cannot imagine the power of the Almighty, yet he is so just and merciful that he does not oppress us. ❖ He will listen to the prayers of the destitute. He will not reject their pleas. (James 5:13-18; Job 42:2; 37:23; Psalm 102:17)

☐ 264 _____

Shout for joy, O heavens; rejoice, O earth; burst into song, O mountains! For the LORD comforts his people and will have compassion on his afflicted ones. ❖ Blessed are the poor in spirit: for theirs is the kingdom of heaven. Blessed are they that mourn: for they shall be comforted. ❖ God shall wipe away all tears from their eyes. (Isaiah 49:13, NIV; Matthew 5:3-4; Revelation 7:17, KJV)

TAKEAWAY
Through cloud and sunshine, Lord, abide with me.—Henry F. Lyte, "Abide with Me"

☐ 265 _____

Uplifting Scriptures to Help Lift Depression: Thy rod and thy staff they comfort me. ❖ Weeping may endure for a night, but joy cometh in the morning. ❖ In God I trust; I will not be afraid. ❖ Now glory be to God, who by his mighty power at work within us is able to do far more than we would ever dare to ask or even dream of—infinitely beyond our highest prayers, desires, thoughts, or hopes. ❖ The LORD is a shelter for the oppressed, a refuge in times of trouble. Those who know your name trust in you, for you, O LORD, have never abandoned anyone who searches for you. ❖ The very hairs on your head are all numbered. (Psalms 23:4; 30:5, KJV; Psalm 56:11, NIV; Ephesians 3:20, TLB; Psalm 9:9-10; Matthew 10:30)

TAKEAWAY
He restoreth my soul. (Psalm 23:3, KJV)

☐ 266 _____

Powerful thoughts: I *know* that my redeemer liveth. ❖ I *know* whom I have believed, and am persuaded that he is able to keep that which I have committed unto him. ❖ [Jesus said,] I am the good shepherd, and *know* my sheep, and am known of mine. ❖ We *know* that the world and the stars—in fact, all things—were made at God's command. ❖ We know that God has chosen you . . . much beloved of God. ❖ I *know* the Lord is always with me. I will not be shaken, for he is right beside me. ❖ This I *know:* God is on my side. ❖ O LORD, you *know* all about this. ❖ Great is the LORD, who enjoys helping his servant. (Job 19:25; 2 Timothy 1:12; John 10:14, KJV; Hebrews 11:3; 1 Thessalonians 1:4, TLB; Acts 2:25; Psalms 56:9; 35:22, 27) (italics for emphasis)

TAKEAWAY
This I *know:* **God is on my side.**

POWERTHOUGHT

If I have faltered more or less
In my great task of happiness;
If I have moved among my race
And shown no shining morning face;
If beams from happy human eyes
Have moved me not; if morning skies,
Books, and my food, and summer rain
Knocked on my sullen heart in vain;—
Lord, thy most pointed pleasure take
And stab my spirit broad awake.

—ROBERT LOUIS STEVENSON
(1850–1894)

Thirty-nine

WHERE ARE YOU WHEN I NEED YOU, GOD?

☐ 267 _____

Thou shalt find him, if thou seek him with all thy heart and with all thy soul. ❖ He shall come down like rain upon the mown grass: as showers that water the earth. (Deuteronomy 4:29; Psalm 72:6, KJV

TAKEAWAY
Thou shalt find him, if thou seek him.

☐ 268 _____

I can never escape from your spirit! I can never get away from your presence! If I go up to heaven, you are there; if I go down to the place of the dead, you are there. If I ride the wings of the morning, if I dwell by the farthest oceans, even there your hand

will guide me, and your strength will support me.
(Psalm 139:7-10)

> TAKEAWAY
> If I ride to the farthest oceans, even there your
> hand will guide me.

☐ 269 _____

Surely the LORD is in this place; and I knew it not.
(Genesis 28:16, KJV)

> TAKEAWAY
> Surely the Lord is in this place.

☐ 270 _____

Upon whom doth not [God's] light arise? ❖ The
eyes of the LORD are in every place, beholding the
evil and the good. (Job 25:3; Proverbs 15:3, KJV)

> TAKEAWAY
> The eyes of the Lord are in every place,
> beholding.

☐ 271 _____

I could ask the darkness to hide me and the light
around me to become night—but even in darkness I
cannot hide from you. To you the night shines as
bright as day. Darkness and light are both alike to
you. (Psalm 139:11-12)

> TAKEAWAY
> God, I can never be lost to your Spirit—even in
> darkness! To you the night shines as bright as day.

☐ 272 _____

I know the Lord is always with me. I will not be shaken, for he is right beside me. (Acts 2:25)

T A K E A W A Y
He is helping me.

☐ 273 _____

I am not alone, because the Father is with me [Jesus]. ❖ O LORD my God, you have done many miracles for us. Your plans for us are too numerous to list. If I tried to recite all your wonderful deeds, I would never come to the end of them. ❖ Our lives are in his hands, and he keeps our feet from stumbling. (John 16:32, KJV; Psalms 40:5; 66:9)

T A K E A W A Y
He holds our lives in his hands.

POWERTHOUGHT We shall never encounter God in the moment when that encounter takes place. It's always after that we can say, "So that strange situation, that impression, that unexplainable event was God."—JACQUES ELLUL, *Living Faith*

Forty

BIBLE PRAYERS FOR
WORRYWARTS

☐ 274 _____

Listen to my cry for help, my King and my God, for
to you I pray. . . . Lead me, O LORD, in your righteousness. . . . Let all who take refuge in you be
glad; let them ever sing for joy. Spread your protection over them, that those who love your name may
rejoice in you. For surely, O LORD, you bless the
righteous; you surround them with your favor as a
shield. (Psalm 5:2, 8, 11-12, NIV)

T A K E A W A Y
Listen to my cry for help, my King and my God.

☐ 275 _____

The heavens declare the glory of God; the skies proclaim the work of his hands. Day after day they pour

forth speech; night after night they display knowledge. There is no speech or language where their voice is not heard. . . . In the heavens he has pitched a tent for the sun, which is like a bridegroom coming forth from his pavilion, like a champion rejoicing to run his course. It rises at one end of the heavens and makes its circuit to the other; nothing is hidden from its heat. ❖ May he give you the desire of your heart and make all your plans succeed. We will shout for joy when you are victorious and will lift up our banners in the name of our God. . . . He answers . . . from his holy heaven with the saving power of his right hand. Some trust in chariots and some in horses, but we trust in the name of the LORD our God. ❖ Be exalted, O LORD, in your strength. (Psalms 19:1-6; 20:4-7; 21:13, NIV)

TAKEAWAY

The heavens declare the glory of God. Be exalted, O Lord!

☐ 276 _____

You give me your shield of victory, and your right hand sustains me; you stoop down to make me great. You broaden the path beneath me, so that my ankles do not turn. . . . The LORD lives! Praise be to my Rock! Exalted be God my Savior! . . . I will sing praises to your name. . . . He shows unfailing kindness to his anointed. ❖ May the words of my mouth and the meditation of my heart be pleasing in your sight, O LORD, my Rock and my Redeemer. (Psalms 18:35-36, 46, 49-50; 19:14, NIV)

May the words of my mouth and the meditation of my heart be pleasing in your sight, O Lord, my Rock and my Redeemer.

□ 277 _____

Keep me safe, O God, for in you I take refuge. . . . You are my Lord; apart from you I have no good thing. . . . I will praise the LORD, who counsels me; even at night my heart instructs me. I have set the LORD always before me. Because he is at my right hand, I will not be shaken. Therefore my heart is glad and my tongue rejoices. (Psalm 16:1-2, 7-9, NIV)

TAKEAWAY
Because he is at my right hand, I will not be shaken.

□ 278 _____

Arise, LORD! Lift up your hand, O God. Do not forget the helpless. . . . You, O God, do see trouble and grief; you consider it to take it in hand. . . . You are the helper of the fatherless. . . . You hear, O LORD, the desire of the afflicted; you encourage them, and you listen to their cry. . . . In the LORD I take refuge. (Psalms 10:12–11:1, NIV)

TAKEAWAY
Arise, Lord! You see trouble and grief; you consider it to take it in hand. You are the helper. In the Lord I take refuge.

_____

There is no one like the God of Israel. He rides across the heavens to help you, across the skies in majestic splendor. The eternal God is your refuge, and his everlasting arms are under you. He thrusts out the enemy before you; it is he who cries, "Destroy them!". . . He is your protecting shield and your triumphant sword! (Deuteronomy 33:26-29)

> TAKEAWAY
> **The eternal God is your refuge, and underneath are the everlasting arms.**

☐ 280 _____

The LORD is my light and my salvation—whom shall I fear? The LORD is the stronghold of my life—of whom shall I be afraid? . . . Though an army besiege me, my heart will not fear. . . . For in the day of trouble he will keep me safe in his dwelling; he will hide me in the shelter of his tabernacle and set me high upon a rock. (Psalm 27:1-5, NIV)

> TAKEAWAY
> **Whom shall I fear? The Lord is the stronghold of my life.**

POWERTHOUGHT The confident "pray-er" goes off alone to kneel before the Lord. A quiet place is created inside himself. He is inside the calm eye of life's storm, despite turbulent circumstances.

Forty-one

BIBLE WORDS TO QUIET MY MIND

☐ 281 _____

The Sovereign LORD is my strength! He will make me as surefooted as a deer and bring me safely over the mountains. (Habakkuk 3:19)

TAKEAWAY
The Lord God will bring me safely over the mountain.

☐ 282 _____

Can you envision Jesus lifting his hand, then invoking this blessing upon you right now? May the Lord bless and protect you; may the LORD's face radiate with joy because of you; may he be gracious to you, show you his favor, and give you his peace. (Numbers 6:24-26, TLB)

May the Lord's face radiate with joy because of you;
may he be gracious to you and show you his favor.

☐ 283 _____

Fix your thoughts on what is true and honorable
and right. Think about things that are pure and
lovely and admirable. Think about things that are
excellent and worthy of praise. (Philippians 4:8)

TAKEAWAY
Think positive thoughts, pure and lovely
thoughts, praise thoughts.

☐ 284 _____

The righteous face many troubles, but the LORD rescues them from each and every one. For the LORD
protects them from harm—not one of their bones
will be broken! (Psalm 34:19-20)

TAKEAWAY
Troubles—the Lord helps in every one.

☐ 285 _____

If God is for us, who can be against us? He who did
not spare His own Son, but delivered Him up for us
all, how shall He not with Him also freely give us
all things? . . . Yet in all these things we are more
than conquerors through Him who loved us.
(Romans 8:31-32, 37, NKJV)

TAKEAWAY
If God is for us, who can be against us?

So I tell you, don't worry about everyday life—
whether you have enough food, drink, and
clothes. Doesn't life consist of more than food and
clothing? Look at the birds. They don't need to
plant or harvest or put food in barns because your
heavenly Father feeds them. And you are far more
valuable to him than they are. Can all your worries
add a single moment to your life? Of course not.
(Matthew 6:25-27)

TAKEAWAY
**Don't worry about things. Will your worries add
a single moment to your life?**

Be still, and know that I am God: I will be exalted
among the heathen, I will be exalted in the earth.
The LORD of hosts is with us; the God of Jacob is
our refuge. (Psalm 46:10-11, KJV)

TAKEAWAY
Be still, and know that I am God.

POWERTHOUGHT In quietness and in confidence shall
be your strength.—Isaiah 30:15, KJV

Forty-two

LIVING IN THE SHADOW OF THE ALMIGHTY

(PEACE FOR AN AGITATED MIND)

☐ 288 _____

Those who live in the shelter of the Most High will find rest in the shadow of the Almighty. This I declare of the LORD: He alone is my refuge, my place of safety; he is my God, and I am trusting him. . . . He will shield you with his wings. He will shelter you with his feathers. His faithful promises are your armor and protection. (Psalm 91:1-4)

TAKEAWAY
We live within the shadow of the Almighty, safely sheltered by God.

☐ 289 _____

I trust in you, O LORD; I say, "You are my God." My times are in your hands. . . . How great is your goodness, which you have stored up for those who fear you . . . on those who take refuge in you. In the shelter of your presence you hide them from the intrigues of men; in your dwelling you keep them safe. . . . Praise be to the LORD. (Psalm 31:14-15, 19-21, NIV)

TAKEAWAY
You are my God. My times are in your hands.

☐ 290 _____

May our Lord Jesus Christ and God our Father, who loved us and in his special favor gave us everlasting comfort and good hope, comfort your hearts and give you strength in every good thing you do and say. (2 Thessalonians 2:16-17)

TAKEAWAY
God . . . our *Father!*

☐ 291 _____

You will keep him in perfect peace, whose mind is stayed on You, because he trusts in You. Trust in the LORD forever. For in YAH, the LORD, is everlasting strength. (Isaiah 26:3-4, NKJV)

TAKEAWAY
Lord, grant us peace; for all we have and are has come from you. (Isaiah 26:12, TLB)

☐ 292 _____

Come unto me, all ye that labour and are heavy laden, and I will give you rest. Take my yoke upon you, and learn of me; for I am meek and lowly in heart: and ye shall find rest unto your souls. For my yoke is easy, and my burden is light. (Matthew 11:28-30, KJV)

TAKEAWAY
Come unto me, all ye that labour and are heavy laden, and I will give you rest.—Jesus

☐ 293 _____

The LORD is close to all who call on him, yes, to all who call on him sincerely. He fulfills the desires of those who fear him; he hears their cries for help and rescues them. (Psalm 145:18-19)

TAKEAWAY
He is close to all who call on him sincerely. Why not call on him right now if you need peace for an agitated mind?

☐ 294 _____

I will make my people strong in my power, and they will go wherever they wish by my authority. I, the LORD, have spoken! (Zechariah 10:12)

TAKEAWAY
The Lord says, "I will make my people strong in my power, and they will go wherever they wish by my authority."

POWERTHOUGHT Some trust in chariots, and some in horses: but we will remember the name of the LORD our God.—Psalm 20:7, KJV

Forty-three

FOR MIDNIGHT
WORRIERS:
PRAISE PRAYERS
FROM THE PSALMS

☐ 295_____

O LORD, our Lord, the majesty of your name fills the
earth! Your glory is higher than the heavens. You
have taught children and nursing infants to give you
praise. They silence your enemies who were seeking
revenge. When I look at the night sky and see the
work of your fingers—the moon and the stars you
have set in place—what are mortals that you should
think of us, mere humans that you should care for us?
For you made us only a little lower than God, and
you crowned us with glory and honor. You put us in
charge of everything you made, giving us authority
over all things—the sheep and the cattle and all the
wild animals, the birds in the sky, the fish in the sea,
and everything that swims the ocean currents.

O LORD, our Lord, the majesty of your name fills the earth! (Psalm 8)

TAKEAWAY
When I begin to worry in the night, then I will begin to praise God.

☐ 296 _____

I praise you, LORD God, with all my heart. You are glorious and majestic, dressed in royal robes and surrounded by light. You spread out the sky like a tent, and you built your home over the mighty ocean. The clouds are your chariot with the wind as its wings. The winds are your messengers, and flames of fire your servants. You built foundations for the earth, and it will never be shaken. You covered the earth with the ocean that rose above the mountains. Then your voice thundered! And the water flowed down the mountains and through the valleys to the place you prepared. . . . You created the moon to tell us the seasons. The sun knows when to set, and you made the darkness. . . . With all my heart I praise you, LORD! I praise you! (Psalm 104:1-8, 19-20, 35, CEV)

TAKEAWAY
I praise you, Lord God, with all my heart.

☐ 297 _____

I will sing to the Lord as long as I live. I will praise God to my last breath! May he be pleased by all these thoughts about him, for he is the source of all my joy. ❖ Hallelujah! Yes, praise the Lord! Praise him in his Temple, and in the heavens he made with mighty power. Praise him for his mighty works. Praise his unequaled greatness. Praise him with the trumpet and with lute and harp. Praise him with the drums and dancing. Praise him with stringed instruments and horns. Praise him with the cymbals, yes, loud clanging cymbals. Let everything alive give praises to the Lord! *You* praise him! Hallelujah! (Psalms 104:33-34; 150, TLB)

TAKEAWAY
Let everything alive give praises to the Lord!
***You* praise him!**

☐ 298 _____

I will praise you, my God and King, and bless your name forever and ever. I will bless you every day, and I will praise you forever. Great is the LORD! He is most worthy of praise! His greatness is beyond discovery! Let each generation tell its children of your mighty acts. I will meditate on your majestic, glorious splendor and your wonderful miracles. Your awe-inspiring deeds will be on every tongue; I will proclaim your greatness. Everyone will share the story of your wonderful goodness; they will sing with joy of your righteousness. The LORD is kind and merciful, slow to get angry, full of unfailing love. The LORD is good to everyone. He showers compassion on all his creation. (Psalm 145:1-9)

TAKEAWAY
The Lord is good to everyone. He showers compassion on all his creation.

With all my heart I will praise you. I will give glory to
your name forever, for you love me so much! You are
constantly so kind! ❖ Come, kneel before the Lord
our Maker, for he is our God. We are his sheep, and
he is our Shepherd. (Psalms 86:12-13; 95:6-7, TLB)

TAKEAWAY

**When I begin to worry in the night, then I will
begin to praise God.**

Our God, you deserve praise. . . . You are strong,
and your mighty power put the mountains in place.
You silence the roaring waves and the noisy shouts
of the nations. . . . You take care of the earth and
send rain to help the soil grow all kinds of crops.
Your rivers never run dry, and you prepare the earth
to produce much grain. . . . Wherever your footsteps touch the earth, a rich harvest is gathered.
Desert pastures blossom, and mountains celebrate.
Meadows are filled with sheep and goats; valleys
overflow with grain and echo with joyful songs. Tell
everyone on this earth to shout praises to God!
(Psalms 65:1, 6–66:1, CEV)

TAKEAWAY

**When I begin to worry in the night, then I will
begin to praise God.**

I run to you, LORD, for protection. . . . You do what
is right, so come to my rescue. . . . Keep me safe. Be

my mighty rock, the place where I can always run for protection. Save me by your command! You are my mighty rock and my fortress. . . . I will praise you, God. . . . You are faithful. . . . I will celebrate and shout, singing praises to you with all my heart. All day long I will announce your power to save. ❖ It is good for me to be near you. I choose you as my protector, and I will tell about your wonderful deeds. (Psalms 71:1-3, 22-24; 73:28, CEV)

TAKEAWAY

When I begin to worry in the night, then I will begin to praise God.

POWERTHOUGHT

Because the road is rough and long,
Shall we despise the skylark's song?
　　　—ANNE BRONTS, *Views of Life*

Forty-four

HELP FOR
HOPELESSNESS

☐ 302 _____

It is written: "No eye has seen, no ear has heard, no mind has conceived what God has prepared for those who love him." (1 Corinthians 2:9, NIV)

TAKEAWAY
No mind can conceive what God has prepared for those who love him.

☐ 303 _____

Be truly glad! There is wonderful joy ahead, even though it is necessary for you to endure many trials for a while. These trials are only to test your faith, to show that it is strong and pure. It is being tested as fire tests and purifies gold—and your faith is far more precious to God than mere gold. So if your faith remains strong after being tried by fiery trials, it will bring you much praise and glory and honor on the day when Jesus Christ is revealed to the whole world. (1 Peter 1:6-7)

TAKEAWAY

There is wonderful joy ahead, even though the going is rough for a while.

☐ 304 _____

The LORD watches over those who fear him, those who rely on his unfailing love. He rescues them from death and keeps them alive in times of famine. We depend on the LORD alone to save us. Only he can help us, protecting us like a shield. (Psalm 33:18-20)

TAKEAWAY

The eyes of the Lord are watching . . . he protects us like a shield.

☐ 305 _____

Your goodness is so great! You have stored up great blessings for those who honor you. You have done so much for those who come to you for protection, blessing them before the watching world. (Psalm 31:19)

TAKEAWAY

You have stored up great blessings for those who trust and reverence you.

☐ 306 _____

Humble yourselves, therefore, under God's mighty hand, that he may lift you up in due time. Cast all your anxiety on him because he cares for you. Be self-controlled and alert. Your enemy the devil prowls around like a roaring lion looking for someone to devour. Resist him, standing firm in the faith, because you know that your brothers throughout the world are undergoing the same kind of sufferings. And the God of all grace, who called you to his eternal glory in Christ, after you have suffered a little while, will himself restore you and make you strong, firm and steadfast. To him be the power for ever and ever. Amen. (1 Peter 5:6-11, NIV)

TAKEAWAY
Your brothers throughout the world are undergoing the same kind of suffering. The God of all grace will restore you.

☐ 307 _____

O my soul, don't be discouraged. Don't be upset. Expect God to act! For I know that I shall again have plenty of reason to praise him for all that he will do. He is my help! He is my God! (Psalm 42:11, TLB)

TAKEAWAY
Expect God to act!

☐ 308 _____

I waited patiently for the LORD to help me, and he turned to me and heard my cry. He lifted me out of the pit of despair, out of the mud and the mire. He set my feet on solid ground and steadied me as I walked along. He has given me a new song to sing, a hymn of praise to our God. Many will see what he has done and be astounded. They will put their trust in the LORD. (Psalm 40:1-3)

TAKEAWAY
He heard my cry. He lifted me out of the pit of despair and set my feet on a hard, firm path and steadied me.

POWERTHOUGHT I have always felt that the moment when you first wake up in the morning is the most wonderful of the 24 hours. No matter how weary or dreary you feel, you possess the certainty that absolutely anything may happen. And the fact that it practically always *doesn't*, matters not one jot. The possibility is always there.—MONICA BALDWIN, *I Leap over the Wall*

Forty-five

HELP FOR THE BROKENHEARTED

☐ 309 _____

The LORD helps the fallen and lifts up those bent beneath their loads.(Psalm 145:14)

> TAKEAWAY
> **The Lord lifts those bent beneath their loads.**

☐ 310 _____

Sing for joy, O heavens! Rejoice, O earth! Burst into song, O mountains! For the LORD has comforted his people and will have compassion on them in their sorrow. ❖ Come, let us return to the LORD! He has torn us in pieces; now he will heal us. He has injured us; now he will bandage our wounds. In just a short time, he will restore us so we can live in his presence. Oh, that we might know the LORD! Let us press on to know him! Then he will respond to us as surely as the arrival of dawn or the coming of rains in early spring. (Isaiah 49:13; Hosea 6:1-3)

TAKEAWAY

The Lord will have compassion upon them in their sorrow. He will set us on our feet again.

☐ 311 _____

The LORD is there to rescue all who are discouraged and have given up hope. The LORD's people may suffer a lot, but he will always bring them safely through. ❖ Shout praises to the LORD! . . . He renews our hopes and heals our bodies. . . . Our LORD is great and powerful! He understands everything. (Psalms 34:18-19; 147:1-5, CEV)

TAKEAWAY

The Lord is there to rescue all who are discouraged and have given up hope.

☐ 312 _____

The LORD opens the eyes of the blind. The LORD lifts the burdens of those bent beneath their loads. The LORD loves the righteous. (Psalm 146:8)

TAKEAWAY

The Lord loves the righteous. He lifts burdens from those bent down beneath their loads.

☐ 313 _____

He has brought me into deep darkness, shutting out all light. . . . He has attacked me and surrounded me with anguish and distress. . . . He has filled me with bitterness. He has given me a cup of deep sorrow to drink. . . . Peace has been stripped away, and I have forgotten what prosperity is. I cry out, "My splendor is gone! Everything I had hoped for from the LORD is lost!". . . Yet I still dare to hope when I remember this: The unfailing love of the LORD never ends! By his mercies we have been kept from complete destruction. Great is his faithfulness; his mercies begin afresh each day. I say to myself, "The LORD is my inheritance; therefore, I will hope in him!" (Lamentations 3:2, 5, 15, 17-18, 21-24)

TAKEAWAY
His lovingkindness begins afresh each day. I continually hope in him.

☐ 314 _____

My servant grew up in the LORD's presence like a tender green shoot, sprouting from a root in dry and sterile ground. There was nothing beautiful or majestic about his appearance, nothing to attract us to him. He was despised and rejected—a man of sorrows, acquainted with bitterest grief. We turned our backs on him and looked the other way when he went by. He was despised, and we did not care. Yet it was our weaknesses he carried; it was our sorrows that weighed him down. And we thought his troubles were a punishment from God for his own sins! (Isaiah 53:2-4)

TAKEAWAY
Jesus knows all about sadness.

LORD, don't hold back your tender mercies from me. My only hope is in your unfailing love and faithfulness. For troubles surround me—too many to count! They pile up so high I can't see my way out. They are more numerous than the hairs on my head. I have lost all my courage. Please, LORD, rescue me! Come quickly, LORD, and help me. . . . As for me, I am poor and needy, but the Lord is thinking about me right now. You are my helper and my savior. Do not delay, O my God. (Psalm 40:11-13, 17)

TAKEAWAY
Problems far too big for me to solve are piled higher than my head. God, you are my helper.

POWERTHOUGHT The LORD is nigh unto them that are of a broken heart; and saveth such as be of a contrite spirit. ❖ Grace be with you, mercy, and peace.—Psalm 34:18; 2 John 1:3, KJV

Forty-six

GOD TAKES CARE OF TOMORROW, TOO

☐ 316 _____

O God, have mercy on me. The enemy troops press in on me. My foes attack me all day long. ❖ Taste and see that the LORD is good. Oh, the joys of those who trust in him! Let the LORD's people show him reverence, for those who honor him will have all they need. Even strong young lions sometimes go hungry, but those who trust in the LORD will never lack any good thing. (Psalms 56:1; 34:8-10)

TAKEAWAY
Those who reverence the Lord will never lack any good thing.

☐ 317 _____

God will take care of your tomorrow too. Live one day at a time. ❖ He is like a father to us, tender and sympathetic to those who reverence him. For he knows we are but dust and that our days are few and brief, like grass, like flowers, blown by the wind and gone forever. But the loving-kindness of the Lord is from everlasting to everlasting to those who reverence him. (Matthew 6:34; Psalm 103:13-18, TLB)

TAKEAWAY
Live one day at a time.

☐ 318 _____

Blessed are those who trust in the LORD and have made the LORD their hope and confidence. They are like trees planted along a riverbank, with roots that reach deep into the water. Such trees are not bothered by the heat or worried by long months of drought. Their leaves stay green, and they go right on producing delicious fruit. (Jeremiah 17:7-8)

TAKEAWAY
Blessed is the man (or woman) who has made the Lord his (her) hope and confidence.

☐ 319 _____

What do you think the Scriptures mean when they say that the Holy Spirit, whom God has placed within us, jealously longs for us to be faithful? He gives us more and more strength to stand against such evil desires. As the Scriptures say, "God sets himself against the proud, but he shows favor to the humble.". . . Draw close to God, and God will draw close to you. . . . When you bow down before the Lord and admit your dependence on him, he will lift you up and give you honor. (James 4:5-10)

TAKEAWAY
The Holy Spirit watches over us with tender jealousy.

☐ 320 _____

Every morning tell him, "Thank you for your kindness," and every evening rejoice in all his faithfulness. . . . The godly shall flourish. . . . For they are transplanted into the Lord's own garden and are under his personal care. Even in old age they will still produce fruit and be vital and green. This honors the Lord and exhibits his faithful care. He is my shelter. There is nothing but goodness in him! (Psalm 92:2, 12-15, TLB)

TAKEAWAY
He is my shelter.

☐ 321 _____

Can all your worries add a single moment to your life? Of course not. And why worry about your clothes? Look at the lilies and how they grow. They don't work or make their clothing, yet Solomon in all his glory was not dressed as beautifully as they are. And if God cares so wonderfully for flowers that are here today and gone tomorrow, won't he more surely care for you? You have so little faith! (Matthew 6:27-30)

TAKEAWAY
God cares so wonderfully for flowers that are here today and gone tomorrow; won't he more surely care for you?

My God is my rock, in whom I take refuge. (Psalm 18:2, NIV)

T A K E A W A Y
My God is my rock, in whom I take refuge.

POWERTHOUGHT It is a mistake to look too far ahead. Only one link of the chain of destiny can be handled at a time.—WINSTON CHURCHILL

The veil that hides the face of the future is woven by the hand of mercy.

Forty-seven

RESTING IN GOD'S PROTECTIVE CARE

☐ 323 _____

Do not be afraid or discouraged, for the LORD is the one who goes before you. He will be with you; he will neither fail you nor forsake you. (Deuteronomy 31:8)

TAKEAWAY
The Lord will go before you.

☐ 324 _____

All those who come and listen and obey me are like a man who builds a house on a strong foundation laid upon the underlying rock. When the flood-waters rise and break against the house, it stands firm, for it is strongly built. (Luke 6:47-48, TLB)

☐ 325 _____

Who will take his stand for me against those who do wickedness? If the LORD had not been my help, my soul would soon have dwelt in the abode of silence. If I should say, "My foot has slipped," Thy lovingkindness, O LORD, will hold me up. When my anxious thoughts multiply within me, Thy consolations delight my soul. . . . The LORD has been my stronghold, and my God the rock of my refuge. (Psalm 94:16-19, 22, NASB)

TAKEAWAY

When my anxious thoughts multiply, God is the rock of my refuge.

☐ 326 _____

The LORD your God is He who fights for you, just as He promised you. So take diligent heed to yourselves to love the LORD your God. (Joshua 23:10-11, NASB)

TAKEAWAY

God is he who fights for you.

☐ 327 _____

Those who trust in the LORD are as secure as Mount Zion; they will not be defeated but will endure forever. Just as the mountains surround and protect

Jerusalem, so the LORD surrounds and protects his people, both now and forever. (Psalm 125:1-2)

TAKEAWAY
Just as the mountains surround and protect Jerusalem, so the Lord surrounds and protects his people.

☐ 328 _____

You hide them in the shelter of your presence, safe from those who conspire against them. You shelter them in your presence, far from accusing tongues. Praise the LORD, for he has shown me his unfailing love. He kept me safe when my city was under attack. . . . So be strong and take courage, all you who put your hope in the LORD! (Psalm 31:20-21, 24)

TAKEAWAY
His never-failing love protects me like the walls of a fort!

☐ 329 _____

Deliver me . . . O my God; set me securely on high. . . . Arouse Thyself to help me. . . . I will watch for Thee, for God is my stronghold. . . . I shall sing of Thy strength; yes, I shall joyfully sing of Thy lovingkindness in the morning, for Thou has been my stronghold, and a refuge in the day of my distress. O my strength, I will sing praises to Thee, for God is my stronghold, the God who shows me lovingkindness. (Psalm 59:1, 4, 9, 16-17, NASB)

God is my stronghold and a refuge in the day of my distress.

POWERTHOUGHT Surely goodness and mercy shall follow me all the days of my life.—Psalm 23:6, KJV

Forty-eight

TEAMING UP WITH GOD: TOGETHER WE CAN HANDLE ANYTHING

☐ 330 _____

Prepare to meet your God as he comes in judgment. . . . For the LORD is the one who shaped the mountains, stirs up the winds, and reveals his every thought. He turns the light of dawn into darkness and treads the mountains under his feet. The LORD God Almighty is his name! (Amos 4:12-13)

TAKEAWAY
I can trust a God like this.

☐ 331 _____

If you want favor with both God and man, and a reputation for good judgment and common sense, then trust the Lord completely; don't ever trust yourself. ❖ Have you ever once commanded the morning to appear and caused the dawn to rise in the east? Have you ever told the daylight to spread to the ends of the earth, to end the night's wickedness? Have you ever robed the dawn in red? . . . Have you explored the springs from which the seas come, or walked in the sources of their depths? (Proverbs 3:4-5; Job 38:12-16, TLB)

> TAKEAWAY
> I can trust the God who is able to command the morning to appear, then robe the dawn in red.

☐ 332 _____

Look, God is all-powerful. Who is a teacher like him? (Job 36:22)

> TAKEAWAY
> My strong and powerful heavenly Father is worthy of my trust.

☐ 333 _____

Oh, that we might know the Lord! Let us press on to know him, and he will respond to us as surely as the coming of dawn or the rain of early spring. ❖ The earth trembles at his glance; the mountains burst into flame at his touch. I will sing to the Lord as long as I live. I will praise God to my last breath! (Hosea 6:3; Psalm 104:32-33, TLB)

> TAKEAWAY
> Press on to know him. To know him is to trust him.

Do you know when the mountain goats give birth?
Have you watched as the wild deer are born? Do you
know how many months they carry their young? Are
you aware of the time of their delivery? They crouch
down to give birth to their young and deliver their
offspring. . . . Are you the one who makes the hawk
soar and spread its wings to the south? Is it at your
command that the eagle rises to the heights to make
its nest? It lives on the cliffs, making its home on a
distant, rocky crag. (Job 39:1-3, 26-28)

T A K E A W A Y
To know God is to trust him.

Who is this that questions my wisdom with such
ignorant words? Brace yourself, because I have some
questions for you, and you must answer them. Where
were you when I laid the foundations of the earth?
Tell me, if you know so much. Do you know how its
dimensions were determined and who did the survey-
ing? What supports its foundations, and who laid its
cornerstone as the morning stars sang together and
all the angels shouted for joy? Who defined the
boundaries of the sea as it burst from the womb, and
as I clothed it with clouds and thick darkness? For I
locked it behind barred gates, limiting its shores. I
said, "Thus far and no farther will you come. Here
your proud waves must stop!" (Job 38:2-11)

T A K E A W A Y
I can trust a God like this.

Can you hitch a wild ox to a plow? Will it plow a field for you? Since it is so strong, can you trust it? Can you go away and trust the ox to do your work? ❖ Can you ensure the proper sequence of the seasons or guide the constellation of the Bear with her cubs across the heavens? Do you know the laws of the universe and how God rules the earth? Can you shout to the clouds and make it rain? Can you make lightning appear and cause it to strike as you direct it? Who gives intuition and instinct? Who is wise enough to count all the clouds? Who can tilt the water jars of heaven, turning the dry dust to clumps of mud? Can you stalk prey for a lioness and satisfy the young lions' appetites as they lie in their dens or crouch in the thicket? Who provides food for the ravens when their young cry out to God as they wander about in hunger? (Job 39:10-11; 38:32-41)

TAKEAWAY

God is so strong; will you trust him?

POWERTHOUGHT God is not nice. He is not an uncle. God is an earthquake.—ABRAHAM HESCHEL

Forty-nine

NO MORE "WHAT IFS?"

☐ 337 _____

Seek the LORD and his strength, seek his face continually. ❖ Blessed be the LORD my strength, which teacheth my hands to war, and my fingers to fight. (1 Chronicles 16:11; Psalm 144:1, KJV)

> *TAKEAWAY*
> **The Lord, my strength, teaches my fingers to fight.**

☐ 338 _____

The Lord is King forever and forever. . . . Lord, you know the hopes of humble people. Surely you will hear their cries and comfort their hearts by helping them. ❖ Be strong, and let your heart take courage, all you who hope in the LORD. (Psalm 10:16-17, TLB; Psalm 31:24, NASB)

TAKEAWAY

Be strong, and let your heart take courage.

☐ 339 _____

Have I not commanded thee? Be strong and of a
good courage; be not afraid, neither be thou dismayed: for the LORD thy God is with thee wither-
soever thou goest. (Joshua 1:9, KJV)

TAKEAWAY

**The Lord thy God is with thee whithersoever
thou goest.**

☐ 340 _____

The LORD hath set apart him that is godly for himself: the LORD will hear when I call unto him. ❖ Call
unto me, and I will answer thee, and shew thee
great and mighty things, which thou knowest not.
(Psalm 4:3; Jeremiah 33:3, KJV)

TAKEAWAY

The Lord will hear when I call unto him.

☐ 341 _____

[Jesus] came to Jacob's Well . . . tired from a long
walk in the hot sun. . . . Soon a Samaritan woman
came to draw water, and Jesus asked her for a drink.
. . . [He told her,] "If you only knew . . . who I am,
you would ask me for some *living* water." "But you
don't have a rope or a bucket," she said, "and this is
a very deep well! Where would you get this living
water?". . . Jesus replied that people soon became
thirsty again after drinking [ordinary] water. "But

the water I give them," he said, "becomes a perpetual spring within them, watering them forever." (John 4:5-7, 10-14, TLB)

TAKEAWAY

Anxiety is the natural result when our hopes are centered in anything short of God and his will for us.—Billy Graham

☐ 342 _____

Norman Vincent Peale suggests practicing the actual "receiving" of the gift of Christ's peace. Do this by repeating Jesus' words, personalized (insert your name in the blanks): "Peace I leave with you, _____ , my peace I give unto you, _____ : not as the world giveth, give I unto you, _____ . Let not _____'s heart be troubled, neither let it be afraid." (John 14:27, KJV)

TAKEAWAY

My peace I give unto you, _____ (insert your name).

☐ 343 _____

The love of God is my pillow,
Soft and healing and wide;
I rest my soul in its comfort,
And in its calm I abide.

—LONG,
in *Our Daily Bread*, March '96

The love of God is my pillow. I rest my soul in its comfort.

☐ 344 _____

> O God, our Help in ages past,
> Our Hope for years to come,
> Our Shelter from the stormy blast,
> And our eternal Home!
>
> Under the shadow of Thy throne,
> Still may we dwell secure;
> Sufficient is Thine arm alone,
> And our defense is sure.
>
> —ISAAC WATTS (1674–1748)

TAKEAWAY
God: Our shelter from the stormy blast.

POWERTHOUGHT Ten thousand difficulties do not make me doubt.—JOHN HENRY NEWMAN

God commands you to pray but forbids you to worry.
—ST. JOHN VIANNEY

Fifty

ATTITUDE ADJUSTERS

☐ 345 _____

They that wait upon the LORD shall renew their
strength; they shall mount up with wings as eagles;
they shall run, and not be weary; and they shall
walk, and not faint. (Isaiah 40:31, KJV)

> TAKEAWAY
> **They that wait upon the Lord shall mount up
> with wings as eagles.**

☐ 346 _____

I will never leave thee, nor forsake thee. (Hebrews
13:5, KJV)

> TAKEAWAY
> **I will never leave you.**

☐ 347 _____

The LORD gave me everything I had, and the LORD has taken it away. Praise the name of the LORD! (Job 1:21)

T A K E A W A Y
The Lord gave me everything I have; all belongs to him.

☐ 348 _____

What time I am afraid, I will trust in thee. ❖ God has not given us a spirit of fear and timidity, but of power, love, and self-discipline. (Psalm 56:3, KJV; 2 Timothy 1:7)

T A K E A W A Y
The spirit of fear does not come from God.

☐ 349 _____

I shall never be moved. LORD, by thy favour thou hast made my mountain to stand strong. ❖ The LORD God is a sun and shield: the LORD will give grace and glory: no good thing will he withhold from them that walk uprightly. (Psalms 30:6-7; 84:11, KJV)

T A K E A W A Y
Lord, thou has made my mountain to stand strong.

☐ 350 _____

He maketh me to lie down in green pastures: he leadeth me beside the still waters. He restoreth my soul. ❖ My presence shall go with thee, and I will give thee rest. ❖ Let the peace of God rule in your hearts. (Psalm 23:2-3; Exodus 33:14; Colossians 3:15, KJV)

TAKEAWAY
He leadeth me beside still waters.

☐ 351 _____

I will fear no evil: for thou art with me. . . . Surely goodness and mercy shall follow me all the days of my life. ❖ The eternal God is thy refuge, and underneath are the everlasting arms. (Psalm 23:4, 6; Deuteronomy 33:27, KJV)

TAKEAWAY
Thou art with me.

POWERTHOUGHT Christianity has died many times and risen again; for it had a God who knew his way out of the grave.—G. K. CHESTERTON

Fifty-one

MIND MENDERS

☐ 352 _____

The LORD looks from heaven; He sees all the sons of men. From the place of His dwelling He looks on all the inhabitants of the earth; . . . He considers all their works. ❖ The LORD is good, a stronghold in the day of trouble; and He knows those who trust in Him. (Psalm 33:13-15; Nahum 1:7, NKJV)

TAKEAWAY
The Lord is a stronghold in the day of trouble.

☐ 353 _____

I keep the LORD always before me; because he is at my right hand, I shall not be moved. (Psalm 16:8, NRSV)

TAKEAWAY
The Lord is at my right hand.

You offer forgiveness, that we might learn to fear you. ❖ You were dead because of your sins and because your sinful nature was not yet cut away. Then God made you alive with Christ. He forgave all our sins. He canceled the record that contained the charges against us. He took it and destroyed it by nailing it to Christ's cross. In this way, God disarmed the evil rulers and authorities. He shamed them publicly by his victory over them on the cross of Christ. (Psalm 130:4; Colossians 2:13-15)

TAKEAWAY

For every child of God defeats this evil world by trusting Christ to give the victory. (1 John 5:4)

□ 355

[The Lord is] like an eagle that stirs up its nest and hovers over its young, that spreads its wings to catch them and carries them on its pinions. (Deuteronomy 32:11, NIV)

TAKEAWAY

Eagle parents are known to catch the young fledglings on their own wings and carry them along until the little ones get the hang of flying.

□ 356

[God] alone is my rock and my salvation, my fortress where I will not be shaken. My salvation and my honor come from God alone. He is my refuge, a rock where no enemy can reach me. O my people, trust in him at all times. Pour out your heart to him, for God is our refuge. (Psalm 62:6-8)

TAKEAWAY

[God] alone is my rock and my salvation, my fortress where I will not be shaken.

☐ 357 _____

All who enter into God's rest will find rest from their labors, just as God rested after creating the world. . . . That is why we have a great High Priest who has gone to heaven, Jesus the Son of God. Let us cling to him and never stop trusting him. This High Priest of ours understands our weaknesses, for he faced all of the same temptations we do, yet he did not sin. So let us come boldly to the throne of our gracious God. There we will receive his mercy, and we will find grace to help us when we need it. (Hebrews 4:10, 14-16)

TAKEAWAY

The Holy Spirit helps us in our distress. For we don't even know what we should pray for, nor how we should pray. But the Holy Spirit prays for us with groanings that cannot be expressed in words. And the Father who knows all hearts knows what the Spirit is saying, for the Spirit pleads for us believers in harmony with God's own will. (Romans 8:26-27)

☐ 358 _____

O God, . . . I am trusting you! I will hide beneath the shadow of your wings until this storm is past. I

will cry to the God of heaven who does such wonders for me. He will send down help from heaven to
save me, because of his love and faithfulness. . . .
O God, my heart is quiet and confident. No wonder I can sing your praises! Rouse yourself, my soul!
Arise, O harp and lyre! Let us greet the dawn with
song! . . . Your kindness and love are as vast as the
heavens. Your faithfulness is higher than the skies.
Yes, be exalted, O God. (Psalm 57:1-3, 7-11, TLB)

TAKEAWAY
**Oh, how great peace and quietness would he pos-
sess who should cut off all vain anxiety and place
all his confidence in God.—Thomas à Kempis
(1380–1471)**

POWERTHOUGHT God works the night shift, too!

Fifty-two

I LOVE YOU, LORD

☐ 359 _____

I will love you, O LORD, my strength. ❖ The one
thing I want from God, the thing I seek most of all,
is the privilege of meditating in his Temple, living
in his presence, every day of my life, delighting in
his incomparable perfections and glory. (Psalm
18:1, NKJV; Psalm 27:4, TLB)

T A K E A W A Y
I love you, O Lord, my strength.

☐ 360 _____

> *Day by day*
> *Dear Lord, of Thee three things I pray:*
> *To see Thee more clearly,*
> *Love Thee more dearly,*
> *Follow Thee more nearly,*
> *Day by day.*
> —ST. RICHARD OF CHICHESTER

Day by day . . . to love Thee, Lord, more dearly,
to follow Thee more nearly. This I pray.

□ 361 _____

Thou preparest a table before me in the presence of
mine enemies: thou anointest my head with oil; my
cup runneth over. (Psalm 23:5, KJV)

T A K E A W A Y
My cup runneth over.

□ 362 _____

I love you, LORD; you are my strength. The LORD is
my rock, my fortress, and my savior; my God is my
rock, in whom I find protection. He is my shield,
the strength of my salvation, and my stronghold. I
will call on the LORD, who is worthy of praise, for
he saves me from my enemies. ❖ As the deer pants
for streams of water, so I long for you, O God. I
thirst for God, the living God. When can I come
and stand before him? (Psalms 18:1-3; 42:1-2)

T A K E A W A Y
As the deer pants for water, so I long for you,
O God.

□ 363 _____

My heart has heard you say, "Come and talk with
me, O my people." And my heart responds, "Lord, I
am coming." ❖ We know how much God loves us
because we have felt his love and because we

believe him when he tells us that he loves us dearly. . . . We need have no fear of someone who loves us perfectly; his perfect love for us eliminates all dread of what he might do to us. . . . So, you see, our love for him comes as a result of his loving us first. (Psalm 27:8; 1 John 4:16-19, TLB)

TAKEAWAY

He loves us dearly. Our love for him comes as a result of his loving us first.

☐ 364 _____

I exist because God is good.—**St. Augustine**

TAKEAWAY

Every man, woman, and child all over the world is feeling and breathing at this moment only because God, so to speak, is "keeping him going."—C. S. Lewis, *Mere Christianity*

☐ 365 _____

My Jesus, I love Thee, I know Thou art mine;
For Thee all the follies of sin I resign;
My gracious Redeemer, my Saviour art Thou;
If ever I loved Thee, my Jesus, 'tis now.

I love Thee, because Thou has first loved me,
And purchased my pardon on Calvary's tree;
I love Thee for wearing the thorns on Thy brow;
If ever I loved Thee, my Jesus, 'tis now.

—WILLIAM R. FEATHERSTONE (1842–1878)

I love you, O Lord, my strength. (Psalm 18:1, NKJV)

POWERTHOUGHT

Nearer, my God, to Thee,
  Nearer to Thee!
E'en though it be a cross
  That raiseth me!
Still all my song shall be,
  Nearer, my God, to Thee;
Nearer, my God, to Thee,
  Nearer to Thee!

—SARAH ADAMS